What Others Are Saying About "The Tall Lady with the Iceberg" (formerly "Metaphorically Selling")

"Successful communicators from Aristotle to Reagan and Clinton have used the wisdom in this book to sell their ideas. This book is the perfect tool for people like you and me when we want to close a deal."

—Michael C. Donaldson, Author
"Negotiating for Dummies"

"Like a hot knife through butter, the ideas in this book will melt away objections and help you spread your ideas further and faster. Don't hesitate...learn what Anne's got to teach."

—Seth Godin, Author
"Purple Cow" and "Free Prize Inside"

"As alluring as ice-cold lemonade when you're standing on Texas asphalt in August heat. Do you see how quickly I learned from this book?! Don't leave home (and go to a client) without it."

—Alan Weiss, Author
"Million Dollar Consulting"

"I sell. I sell million dollar consulting contracts to skeptical CEO's. I sell change programs to reluctant managers. I sell books and articles to editors with small obsidian where their hearts should be. And I learned how to communicate and sell by listening to Anne Miller. For twenty years, I have found her counsel to be relevant and useful. This book is no exception. It has pride of place on my bookshelf."

—Sam Hill, Author
"Radical Marketing" and "Sixty Trends in Sixty Minutes"

"If—as Anne Miller says—a metaphor is a 'short-cut to instant understanding,' then this book is a short cut to instant improvement for the sales professional. Metaphors have the power to package big ideas and help them break through the clutter and indifference of our A.D.D. business climate. Anne puts that power into the hands of all sellers...and there aren't metaphors strong enough to describe the impact."

—Doug Weaver, Lecturer, Trainer, Consultant,
President Upstream Group

"The use of appropriate timely, tasteful and powerful metaphorical illustrations are the poetry of all superb communicators. Anne shows how to use metaphors to dramatize the sales process. A must read to help you become a superlative persuader."

—Tony Whatley, President
Accessor Capital Management

"Anne Miller is one of those people who fully understands the sales process and what works and what doesn't. There are sales books and there are sales books. This is the top of the list. It's real, to the point, a fun read, and it works."

—Richard Kinsler, President, SLG Advertising
(former Publisher, "New York Magazine")

"Once again, Anne Miller applies her unmatched insight, clarity, and approachability to drive home the science of selling. Metaphorically Selling is a compelling must for all persuaders."

—Kevin Allen, Chief Collaboration Officer
Interpublic Group, Inc.

"After reading this book, you will add the strategic use of metaphors to the musts of your high stake selling efforts. Anne focuses our attention on this powerful sales tool in a way that most of us don't really stop and think about. This book and its tips will help all of us in business, whether you are directly involved in sales or not and at any experience level."

—Jill Manee, Vice President, Publisher
The AdAge Group

Other Books by Anne Miller

Make What You Say Pay! (Chiron)
365 Sales Tips for Winning Business (Perigee)
Presentation Jazz! How to Make Sales Presentations $ing (Amacom)

Online Newsletter

The Metaphor Minute (www.annemiller.com)

The Tall Lady with the Iceberg

The Power of Metaphors to Sell, Persuade, & Explain Anything to Anyone

Second Edition

Anne Miller

Chiron Associates, Inc.
New York

Second Edition: October 2012

ISBN: 978-0-9762794-4-0 (print)
ISBN: 978-0-9762794-7-1 (epub)
ISBN: 978-0-9762794-8-8 (epdf)

Library of Congress Control Number: 2004114293

Credits:
Cartoon icons: Steve Martinez
S.M.Kreations
Sherman Oaks, CA 91411
Cover designer: bill@billjeckells.com

Available online and in bookstores.
For quantity orders and discounts, call: 800-247-6553

For

Mark, Cara,

Morgan, & Daisy

Table of Contents

Note to Expanded Edition xiii
Introduction: The $1.2 Billion Metaphor 1

SECTION ONE: The Case for Metaphor

Chapter 1: The Challenge: Getting Heard 7
Chapter 2: What Are Metaphors? 13
Chapter 3: When Do You Need Metaphors? 25
Chapter 4: Your Audience's Brain Craves Metaphors 27

SECTION TWO: Building Metaphor Muscle

Chapter 5: The Four-Step Metaphor Workout: Overview . . 41
Chapter 6: Identify Blindspot 45
Chapter 7: Snapshot Your Client 51
Chapter 8: Create Your Metaphor 55
Chapter 9: Relate Back to Your Point 59
Chapter 10: Beware Bad Metaphors! 61

SECTION THREE: Selling with Metaphors

Chapter 11: Threads: Run a Theme 67
Chapter 12: Grabbers: Get Attention 71
Chapter 13: Anchors: Position Yourself 79
Chapter 14: Nutshells: Make Memorable Recommendations 85
Chapter 15: Burners: Explain, Simplify, Reinforce Points . . . 87
Chapter 16: Shockers: Make Numbers Stick 99
Chapter 17: Seducers: Titles That Tease 105
Chapter 18: Sledgehammers: Headlines That Hit Home . . . 111
Chapter 19: To Communicate Concepts 115
Chapter 20: Props: Add Impact 121
Chapter 21: Clinchers: For Dramatic Take-Action Closings . . 127

SECTION FOUR: Metaphor Maintenance

Chapter 22: Observe and Connect 133
Chapter 23: Travel to Other Worlds 137
Chapter 24: Become a Clipper 141

Conclusion 161

Appendix: 25 Stories from Metaphorians Like You 163

Chapter Notes 201

Bibliography 204

Other Sources of Interest 206

About Anne Miller 207

Acknowledgments

My interest in metaphors and analogies as powerful sales and communications tools goes back many years. Traveling from interest to a practical business book, however, was a long road that took many twists and turns and involved many people. First and foremost, I want to thank Melinda Marshall, my superb editor who, with her wit, grace and patience, helped shape my words and thoughts into a lively, useful manuscript for you, my reader.

When friends and clients heard about this project, they were eager to contribute and many acted as early soundboards for my ideas. My thanks to the highly accomplished experts, for whom I have the greatest admiration, who so kindly endorsed this book. Additional thanks to Sue Agresta, James Dawson, Debra Pickrel, Helen DiStefano, Mary Ann Doggett, Jim Donoghue, Marcia Grace, Josh Hammond, Lisa Gilbert, Jay Miller, Ilene Rapkin, Steve Rivkin, Carol Terakawa, Rick Trout, and Joy Wheeler for their generous input as well.

My wonderful supportive family encouraged me throughout this project and to them I say a loving "Thank you."

Finally, my enthusiastic gratitude to all the metaphor makers whose writings, presentations, and speeches have provided the treasure trove of examples in this book.

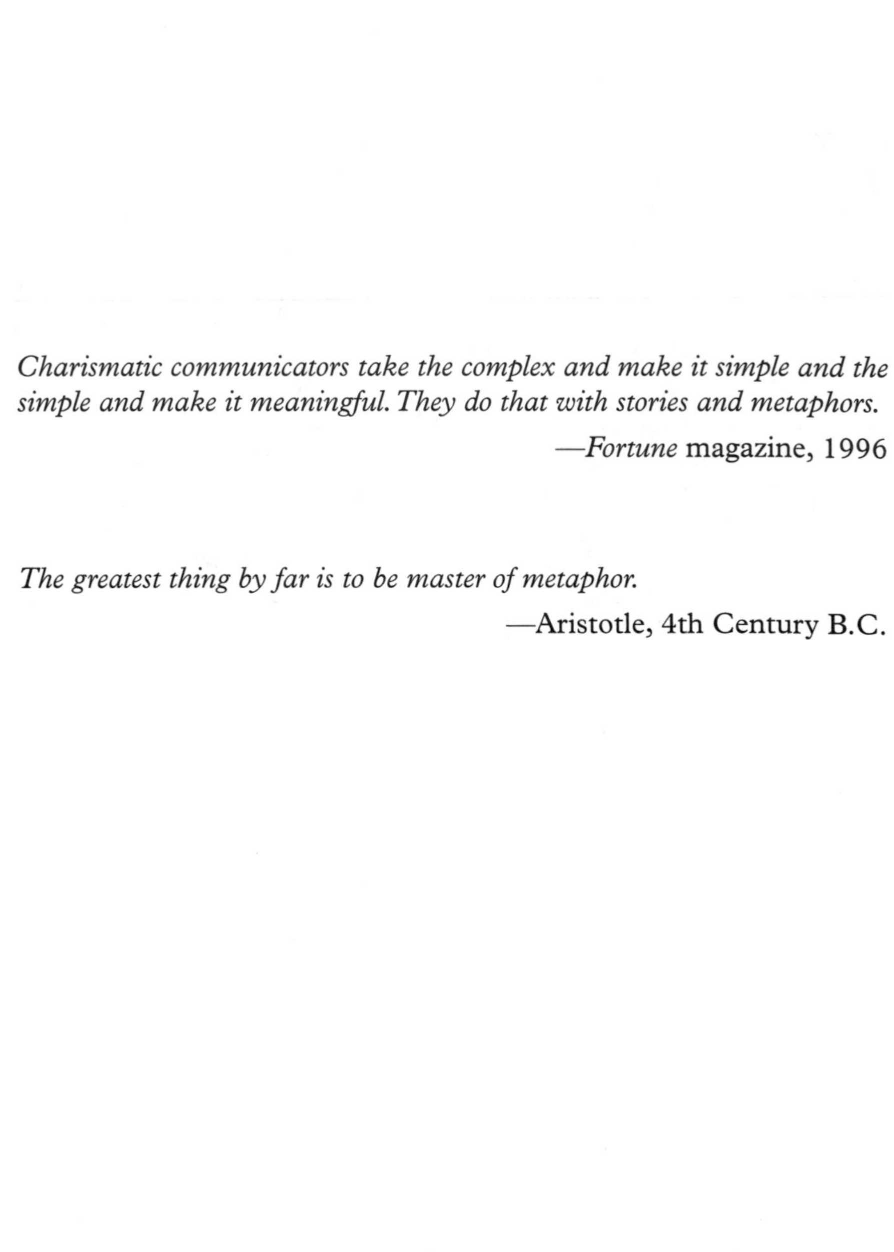

Charismatic communicators take the complex and make it simple and the simple and make it meaningful. They do that with stories and metaphors.

—*Fortune* magazine, 1996

The greatest thing by far is to be master of metaphor.

—Aristotle, 4th Century B.C.

Note to Expanded Edition

As soon as you move one step up from the bottom, your effectiveness depends on your ability to reach others through the spoken and written word.

—Peter Drucker

When you run into someone you recognize at the airport or on the street, but you can't immediately identify them, and you frantically try to figure out how you know them, what's going through your mind?

A. A list of words?
B. A column of numbers?
C. A rush of images?

Answer: "C." A rush of images.

Ultimately and triumphantly, you burst out with something like, "I know you! I know you! You sat next to me in law school!" Or, "We were in day camp together when we were five!" Or, "You're the tall lady with the iceberg!" (More about that a little later.)

We Are Image Junkies

Our brains are wired to respond to imagery. We notice images. We remember in images. We have emotional reactions to images. We make decisions based on images. We talk in images. For centuries, mankind's communications have reflected this primal reach for images to communicate.

Sometimes, the images are actual pictures. Other times, they are expressed in language that is vivid and pictorial, which creates mental images for listeners.

- Cavemen used wall paintings to tell stories of their lives.
- Aesop and Grimm entertained and taught with images in their fairy tales.
- Every religion is rich with images to support its meaning and power.

- Aristotle noted, "To be master of metaphor [word images] is everything."
- Poets capture imaginations with imagery: "My love is like a red, red rose."
- Advertisers sell products with images. Find a car ad without the car in it.
- Brands use images to identify themselves. Take your pick—from the Nike Swoosh to the Geico lizard to Apple's ... well, apple.
- Politicians manipulate the public with images: Willy Horton, Axis of Evil, The Great Society, Contract with America, the Tea Party.
- Corporations construct their cultures around story images: Microsoft's two guys tinkering in a garage; Ivory soap "so pure it floats," early Post-It Notes as bookmarks, Nordstrom's superb customer service—so superb, in fact, that they allowed a customer to return tires when the store doesn't even sell tires.
- The Internet uses images to make it user-friendly: Web, Desktop, Trash Can, Folders, Virus.
- Wall Street uses images as shorthand to describe market behavior and dynamics: Bulls, bears, spiders, poison pills, white knights.
- Finally, our daily conversations are peppered with images: "Not enough bandwidth to process that." "The market is going off a cliff." "It's apples and oranges." "It's a jungle out there."

Even Einstein acknowledged the centrality images play in how we process information: "If I can't see it, I don't understand it."

Why This Update

Since the first edition of this book appeared in late 2004, originally titled *Metaphorically Selling,* the world has become a noisier place. Competition for our attention, loyalty, and commitment has skyrocketed. A numbing stream of 24/7 information delivered on a proliferation of sophisticated electronic gadgets, an explosion of similar-looking products and services, and a tough economy that can induce inertia—all these factors have made people even more inclined to tune out what you have to say. Never before has it been so hard to get and keep someone's attention.

But we still have to get things done.

I have seen my clients twist themselves into knots, trying to keep their audiences tuned in to their speeches, their clients responsive to their pitches, their colleagues attentive to deadlines. The need to deploy metaphoric language in order to influence thinking, shape opinions, change minds, and simply get things done in business has never been greater.

So I decided to re-issue *Metaphorically Selling* with a fresh title and a new Appendix of expanded stories and Take-Away Tips.

The original chapters and "Your Turn" sections of this book remain as valid and useful as they were when they were first published. They will help you develop your metaphorical language skills.

The new Appendix of stories from readers and the additional Take-Away Tips will further inspire you to incorporate metaphors into your world.

Throughout this book, I have used "metaphor" and "metaphorical" in the broadest sense to include all of the following:

- Metaphors
- Analogies
- Stories
- Anecdotes
- Cartoons
- Slide images
- Props

These visual communication tools, when used strategically, will help you capture attention, amplify meaning, clarify complexity, and create powerful reactions in anyone—including clients, customers, bosses, employees, colleagues, and just about every other member of the human race.

Why *The Tall Lady with the Iceberg?*

As I was searching for a stronger, more visual title for this book than *Metaphorically Selling II*, the current title came to me. In my "Present Like a Pro" and "Got Metaphor?" seminars and speeches, I lead a number of quick exercises and games to illustrate how our brains are wired to respond more to images than just words alone.

One of these exercises shows a typical PowerPoint slide with six simple bullet points of text. The slide deals with the present and future services of computer telephony. The information on the slide lists the services we have today followed by a list of services consumers will enjoy tomorrow.

First, I present the message of the slide. Then I show the slide again, but this time with an image of an iceberg alongside the text, and I say: "The services we have today are just the tip of the iceberg. But the services below the waterline, the ones still being developed, will really change the industry."

Then I ask the group which slide resonates more with them. Invariably, without exception, they choose the second one—because of the iceberg image. I make the point that even without the image itself, just talking about an iceberg while showing the data would create the same resonance in listeners, because *in their minds* they will "see" the image that the word creates.

To underscore the point that we are all wired for images, I often tell my clients, "Five years from now, if you see me walking down the street, you will probably not remember my name, but I guarantee you will remember me as the tall lady with the iceberg." (I am 5'11") They laugh, recognizing how true that is.

Once you discover your inner "Metaphorian," it will forever change and improve the way you communicate.

Go forth, imagine, and prosper.

"The mind never thinks without a picture."

—Aristotle

Introduction

The $1.2 Billion Metaphor

IN 1980, LEE IACOCCA went to Congress to get $1.2 billion in loan guarantees for the then failing Chrysler Corporation. Congress was not interested in a bailout, which is how it perceived the loan. Iacocca cleverly changed that perception by substituting the image "safety net" for "bail out." He argued, quite successfully, that the government provided all kinds of safety nets for its citizens and that Chrysler, with all its employees, represented a large group of citizens. Chrysler's problems were America's problems; Chrysler's bankruptcy would be America's loss.

No congressperson wanted to be accused of denying hardworking Americans a safety net. Iacocca got his money.

There's a proverb that says one tiny little word can be a clap of thunder. Iacocca's one small phrase won him $1.2 billion dollars. With "safety net," he shifted the public's perception of the guarantee. It wasn't about giving money to the undeserving; it wasn't about hardworking taxpayers bailing out the shiftless. It wasn't even about money, the way Iacocca put it: Congress was to think of it in terms of other safety nets they extended to protect children, feed the homeless, and give a leg up to the temporarily downtrodden.

Lee Iacocca understood the power of metaphors, visual words that conjure an image in the listener's mind and unleash a torrent of associations. With "safety net," Iacocca made Congress see the benefits of a loan just as clearly as they could imagine a great nylon net saving a circus performer who made one little misstep. From a position of resistance, Congress moved to understanding and, ultimately, to acceptance.

That is the power of speaking metaphorically: You can change minds. You can change minds to the tune of *over a billion dollars.* If you're in the business of selling—and who isn't?—then this is a skill you must acquire. The bad news is that millions, if not billions, of dollars are left on the table every day by presenters—everyone from salespeople to CEOs—for lack of just the right metaphor. The good news is you can learn how to use metaphors to move your listener from a position of staunch resistance to eager complicity. Getting your client to yes is much easier with metaphors and much easier to do than you may think.

This book will show you how.

Metaphors Set You Apart

Helen DiStefano, super saleswoman for *Business Week*, participated in one of my seminars which included a discussion of the power of metaphors to sell, explain, and wow in business. Afterward, she said, "This is terrific. Is there a book on this?"

There wasn't and there isn't. Until now.

In my 20 years of teaching sales and presentation seminars, one key factor that I see repeatedly sets sellers apart from their competition is their choice and use of words. Your firm, your product, or your services may not in fact be unique or distinctive, but the way in which you present them can be. When you're trying to sell something—and whenever you are in the position of wanting a result from any constituency, you're selling something—what you say to your client must penetrate and resonate in his mind and ultimately move him to action. It is not enough to present; you must communicate.

And that's why I've written this book: Effective communicators like Lee Iacocca are those who choose their words carefully and who make masterful use of metaphors. What they say isn't just heard; their clients really see what they mean. What they explain doesn't just make sense; it stands out. What they recommend isn't just remembered; it leads to action.

Metaphors Promote Client Relationships

The mantra chanted in the halls of every company these days is "customer focus." In your company, it might be called "client-centered" or "relationship" selling. But it boils down to the same thing: respecting your client, knowing his business, listening to his needs and wants, anticipating new needs, responding with appropriate value-added solutions, and making it easy for him to deal with you and your firm. Clients do business with—and continue to give their business to—those who they believe have taken the trouble to see their concerns from their point of view.

Creating metaphors is by definition client centered, since its starting point is the client's current perception. Metaphors help a client see possibilities he didn't see before and they help him make the best decision. By packaging an idea in highly vivid language, they help him pitch it internally. They help the client feel good about an idea or decision. And that keeps a client coming back.

How To Use This Book

SECTION ONE of this book makes the case for metaphors: what they are, when to use them and why your clients actually want and need you to use them. You'll learn that the brain actually craves the visual and the emotional; that you must appeal to both the left and right sides of your client's brain to make a sale. After you read this section, you'll never want to make another pitch without being prepared with targeted metaphors.

SECTION TWO shows you how to create winning metaphors. The four-step workout will focus you on your client—his needs, his concerns, his experience—so that you can come up with comparisons he can best relate to. By the end of this section, you'll be well on your way to becoming a master of metaphor.

SECTION THREE shows you how to harness the power of metaphors throughout the sales/presentation process. You'll see how metaphors make attention-getting openers. You'll see how to use them to position your services, distinguish your products, explain your ideas, make your points, and ward off objections. You'll learn how metaphors can help you summarize, and move your client to action. You'll be challenged to apply what you've learned in this section with exercises geared to real-world situations.

SECTION FOUR will help you sustain your competitive communication edge with more exercises and tips.

Section One
The Case for Metaphor

"We're fighting like—well, we're fighting."

Chapter 1

The Challenge: Getting Heard

WHAT DO YOU SELL? Intangibles such as management consulting or financial services? Products like silicon chips or office furniture? The worthiness of political or social causes? The marketability of your ideas? Yourself as a candidate for public office?

Say you sell advertising space for a leading business magazine. Every week you visit media planners, corporate advertising directors and marketing management to extol the virtues of your particular publication. Do these buyers listen to what you have to say and then respond, "Great! Here's my money. In fact, I am going to put all my advertising in your magazine!"

Hardly.

Now, be brutally honest about your rate of success out there. On a scale of 1 to 10, with 1 indicating "Not at All" and 10 indicating "Very," to what extent do you meet resistance to the idea, service, or product you're pitching? On the same scale, how easily can your client distinguish you from your competition?

Unless you are selling the cure for cancer, the answer to the Middle East crisis, or a newly discovered oil field under Nebraska, I'd bet you're meeting quite a bit of resistance. Your clients have heard it all, and continue to hear more of it, every day, until you and your competition are utterly indistinguishable. To quote Professor Harold Hill in The Music Man, "Well, ya got trouble, my friend. Right here, I say trouble right here in River City."

Words Matter

As an executive coach and seminar leader, I can say with excellent authority that what passes for communication today, sadly, is often beyond dreadful. It's not that presenters aren't prepared: they know their material, they've worked up a slick PowerPoint presentation, they've got excellent hand-outs. But their verbal skills and/or approach to communicating cost them their audience. They confuse information with communication.

People tend to make two mistakes. The first is that, rather than choose their words carefully, they inundate their listener with everything they know—often speaking more from their point of view rather than from their client's vantage point and doing it far too casually. They put their buyers to sleep. How often have you encountered, for instance, one of these "Sorry Seven"? (How often have you been one of them?)

1. **Stuart Allstylenosubstance:** *Let me wow you with my fancy visuals as I tell you how you're gonna love this!*
2. **Virginia Valleyspeak:** "Like, this product is really good, because, like, it saves you all kinds of time and things, and like, you know, it's competitively priced, uh, and also, you know, it's, uh,..."
3. **Bonnie Bubblegum:** "Our programs are so great! And wait until you meet our team. They are just awesome. And our design is soooo cool. And our process is really neat."
4. **Wally Wallpaper:** "We offer quality service, proven experience, and innovative thinking." (No one ever says, "Our service is about average. Our experience is mixed. And, sometimes we come up with a good idea, but not too often." Now, that would get a client's attention!)
5. **Donna Data-Death:** "On this page is a pie chart showing our distribution of accounts by category. Thirty percent are in pharmaceuticals. Twenty-four percent are in travel. Sixteen percent are in real estate. Fifteen percent are in financial and fifteen are miscellaneous. On the next page are these categories by revenue. Thirty-five percent pharmaceuticals, twenty-five percent financial, twenty-five percent travel, twelve percent real estate and three percent miscellaneous. And on the next page is another page about this breakdown."
6. **Willie Windbag:** "We will provide you with an integrated, digital, functionally parallel, global knowledge databank that synergistically empowers your network while incrementally enhancing your client relationship initiatives without negatively impacting your geographically dispersed human capital."

7. **Darren Doublespeak:** "We've entered a period of retrenchment that will necessitate continued downsizing and greater efficiency in our human resource capacity." (Translation: Business is bad, people are getting fired, and everyone still left with a job will be working overtime to keep it.)

The bet these salespeople make is that something out of their barrage of words will get through, something will stick. In fact just the opposite happens: listeners double their resistance to the message. They cut short the salesperson who is not concise; they tune out the presenter who shovels on the details. The window of opportunity in terms of getting their attention, opening up their minds, and teaching them something they didn't know has never been great, and given the dire state of communication today it is narrowing all the time.

Which brings us to the second reason my clients fail: Too much other information competes for their listeners' attention. Listeners, already drowning in a tidal wave of information, simply can't respond to another similar sounding bucketful thrown in their faces.

We live in an information age. Presumably that means each of us can arm ourselves with whatever information we need, when we need it, to make a sound decision or judgment. But, in fact, we are so awash in info-bits that, instead of feeling better able to discern differences and make decisions, we're drowning in choices. We shut out more stimuli in self-defense.

Think about it. You can't just go into a store and buy aspirin for your headache; there's an entire aisle devoted to pain relief, with no fewer than 22 products vying to be your cure. Been to Starbucks lately? You could have a tall decaffeinated mocha chai with skim milk, an iced grande cappuccino with regular milk, a regular mild Brazil Ipanema Boubon with 2%, or a bold, black, iced Komoto Dragon Blend—and that's just today's offering. Try buying a digital camera to show friends and family how cute your newborn is. There are at least 28 different models to consider, each to be judged on 10 different criteria if you want to make the smartest choice. (By the time you figure out which model to buy, your kid could be in college.) Not even water is simple anymore. In addition to good old tap water and bottled water like Poland Spring and Evian, get ready for the "enhanced" options coming your way: DNA Alcoholic Fruit and Spring Water (carbonated, 5% alcohol content from fruit-wine ingredient); Reebok

Fitness Water (four vitamins, three minerals, electrolytes, fruit flavoring); and Water Joe (up to as much caffeine as a cup of coffee) and others with different mixes of other ingredients.

In fact, there is nowhere you can turn to escape the barrage of pitches vying for your attention and your disposable income. Twenty-five hundred bids for our attention bombard us daily, from the television, the radio, the newspaper, and the Web; from the sides of buildings, buses and river barges; from behind home plate at sports stadiums to the floors of supermarkets. You can't even go to a movie without paying for the privilege of seeing more ads and "fun facts." Product placement ensures you will see commercials in the movies themselves (see Tom Hanks carrying a FedEx package while he just happens to drink his Coca Cola and gets into a new oh-look-it's-a-Lexus car). Coming soon are "moviemercials," movies built around products like G.I. Joe and Hot Wheels. And last, but not least, an ad agency called Flush Media is putting ads in bathrooms. Look for background advertising music and interactive posters in the next restroom stall you enter (the mind boggles at the nature of the "interaction").

The upshot of this glut, of course, is that every pitch, every bid for our attention begins to sound or look the same. I'm the best. I'm not like the others. I have the better argument. I give more value. I have better performance.

Saying more, or speaking louder, won't get you heard amidst this terrific static. You're fighting for a shrinking piece of your client's attention. As one of my clients at DoubleClick once said, "I don't have enough bandwidth to hear any more information." In fact, to get through to your client, you don't want your words heard so much as you want them seen.

Visual Words Matter Most

The words that work are those which make your listener experience something: See it, feel it, maybe even hear or taste or smell it. What you say must give your listener a visual, because the visual triggers a raft of meaningful associations. Would you pay $30 to eat a piece of dead steer meat? Unlikely. But you do just that when you order filet mignon, a description which conjures quite a different set of associations in your mind. (1) Frequently in fact, you buy something on the strength of a description that isn't accurate so much as it is visually and viscerally enticing.

Words that trigger a gut reaction can be quite subtle; you may be hardly conscious of their inherent power. In one experiment demonstrating just how subtly word choice can affect our perception, a group of people were shown a picture of an automobile accident and then asked individually, "How fast were the cars going when they _______?" With each person a different verb filled in the blank: "bumped," "contacted," "hit," "collided," or "smashed." Those who were asked the question with the word "smashed" gave the highest estimates of speed.[2]

Think about what would appeal to you most: a product or service that would help increase your sales or help *catapult, jumpstart, galvanize, trigger, swell, ignite, turbo-charge, electrify,* or *enhance* your sales?

The difference between the right word and the almost right word is the difference between lightning and a lightning bug.

—Mark Twain

When you sell with lightning language, you make people see what you mean in a very persuasive way. In a sales situation, with vivid comparisons you paint positive pictures, trigger meaningful memories, and involve your client.

When Steve Jobs was courting a wavering John Sculley from Pepsi to become CEO of Apple, his winning argument was not a list of facts and benefits. It was the choice of images he famously painted in Sculley's mind when he asked: "Do you want to spend the rest of your life selling sugared water or do you want a chance to change the world?"

Imagery—the core of metaphoric language—will surprise, grab, inform, and persuade your listeners as mere explanation will not. Vivid language will distinguish you from the swarm, will make you heard above the drone, will make you that rare person today: a communicator who gets results. And in our world of information overload, that gives you a tremendous competitive advantage.

Chapter 2

What Are Metaphors?

A METAPHOR IS SIMPLY a way of communicating. It's a shortcut to instant understanding. Think of it as a mental equation in which something is compared to something else. Metaphors make complex and unfamiliar things or ideas simple and familiar to the listener, because they compare the unknown to what the listener already knows and accepts.

Metaphors are as old as Aristotle and as modern as the internet. Presidents use them for persuasion (Lincoln: A house divided against itself cannot stand) and to start wars (the domino theory for Vietnam). Scientists use them to explain phenomena (the atom as a universe). Poets use them imaginatively (Juliet is the sun). Wall Street uses them to describe investors (bulls, bears). And people in business, like Iacocca, use them as the ultimate persuasion tool.

Metaphors are visual in nature and literally help your client or audience "see in a flash" in a vivid, emotional way what you mean. The result is a fresh perspective in your client's mind, one capable of changing a negative reaction such as, "You're too expensive," to a positive "Where do I sign?"

If you were to create an equation for the power of metaphors, it would be:

Information + Metaphor = "I see what you mean!"

General Eisenhower to soldier: ***"Sarge, give me an assessment of the military situation."***
Soldier: ***"Sir, picture a doughnut. We're the hole."***[1]

Strictly speaking, a metaphor creates an image by stating that one thing is the other. "John is a pig" is a metaphor. "Joan is the Queen of quantum theory" is a metaphor. In this book, to simplify matters, I'm going to use the term metaphor to mean any comparison that creates an "aha!" in your client's mind.

The simplest metaphor is a straightforward substitution. This kind of comparison works best if either you build up to it or follow it with a little amplification. For instance, you may explain that you passed over a staffer for a promotion where sensitivity and teamwork were essential to success because he was unpredictable, blunt, and too self-centered. You could conclude with the metaphor, "He's too much of of a loose cannon to risk making him into a team leader."

The more specific your comparison, the more impressions it will conjure up. "Loose cannon" is descriptive, and visual, and even auditory. You could make your point equally well by comparing that staffer to *an actual person* who was notoriously independent, flamboyant, and unpredictable. For example, you could say of this staffer, "He is the 'Donald Trump' of the department." If you've ever described anyone as the "Tiger Woods" of his business, or a regular "Scrooge" when it came to budgets, or the "Martha Stewart" of precision, you've practiced this sort of shorthand. The substitution of a *specific* person/place/thing has the power to conjure a whole constellation of qualities meaningful to your listener.

Another type of metaphor is a substitution using the words "like" or "as." This is a simile, as you may remember from English class. It has slightly less power in terms of the image it creates. When you hear "John is a pig" (direct substitution), you get a very powerful negative image in your mind (no dinner invitations for John!). When you hear "John is like a pig," you may invite him to dinner, but you may also decide not to serve any finger food or sauces that can splash out of his plate. Other examples of similes:

It's like shoveling sand with a fork.
That sports car accelerates like a cheetah.
He's as angry as a wounded bull.

Similes may not be as strong as direct substitutions, but that doesn't mean they don't pack punch. I notice in my presentation skills seminars that people have a deep-seated need to restate almost their entire presentations in their summaries. I tell them that if they haven't made their point by the time they get to the summary, they are unlikely to make the sale in those last thirty seconds. "Summaries are like perfume or cologne." I say. "Less is better." They get it—and they edit.

Being chairman of the Senate Commerce Committee is like being a mosquito in a nudist colony.

—Senator John McCain on the prospect of holding polluters and fat cats accountable in his role as Chairman of the Commerce Committee[2]

If you take a comparison and make it relevant on more than one level, you are making what is called an analogy. You can draw analogies to anything: an experience (raising kids); an animal, a person, or thing; a process; a joke or funny observation; a story, fable, or myth. The list of sources for your comparisons is practically endless. When asked to describe what it was like to take his company public and make $28 million, Nico Nierenberg replied, "I think the metaphor is childbirth. It was painful as hell, but when it's over, you say, "Ahh, that wasn't too bad."[3] The important thing to bear in mind is that the substitution (and all its attributes) be utterly known to your listener. You want him to experience a brilliant flash of recognition, not a dim flicker.

My role is that of a grain of sand to the oyster. We've got to irritate Washington a little bit.

—Ross Perot[4]

Say you need to explain how risk correlates to reward when it comes to investing in bankrupt companies. How do you show people something so abstract? "The Wall Street Journal" hit upon just the right analogy:

> *When you buy a lottery ticket, typically you put out fifty cents or a dollar and the payout for those who win is a big hit. People who invest in bankrupt companies are looking for that kind of hit.*[5]

In her speeches, Dr. Rachel Ehrenfeld, author of "Funding Evil," and Director of NY based American Center for Democracy, invokes the image and behavior of an unseen enemy with this analogy:

> *Terrorism is like an octopus. You can cut off one leg, one terrorist group, but it will grow back, plus there are seven other legs that can hurt you. What you have to do is kill the octopus by starving it, taking away its food. And with terrorists that means starving them of money. If we fail to starve the octopus, it will strangle us.*

And breathes there a sales manager who hasn't borrowed the philosophy of Green Bay Packers' coach Vince Lombardi when arguing the need for periodic sales training? "It's like football," said Lombardi. "It isn't about being fancy. It's about the basics. If you block and tackle better than your opponent, you win championships." ("Therefore, like the Packers, we are having a training session to practice our basics so that we can win over our competition…")

Many analogies draw on stories. The listener forgets what he thinks you're going to say and listens, rapt, to something he didn't expect. He's transported, briefly, by your extended metaphor, your story, your joke—and that may give you the breakthrough you seek. I know a number of sales reps who have answered a client's question, "Why should I use your service/product?" with this unexpected story:

Do you know who Willie Sutton was? No?
Well, Willie was a bank robber. When he was asked why he robbed banks, he replied, 'Because that's where the money is!' Mr. Client, this product /service is where the money is as well…

When Jack Viertel, artistic director of New York's City Center Encores! was describing music, he might just as well have been describing the effect of metaphors and analogies. "It's almost like magic. The music somehow reaches right past your intellectual faculties and sticks its fingers on some kind of joy buzzer inside your brain that isn't strictly driven by logic."[6]

Metaphors? Me? You're Joking!

Absolutely not. If you're thinking you aren't poetic or creative enough to come up with winning metaphors, you're wrong. You already speak in metaphors and analogies. You reach for them all the time in daily conversation to describe people, situations, feelings, and events. Just try to get through the day without them. You can't. When you "chew" on an idea, "plow" through your work, return a "mountain" of phone messages, check your "inbox" emails, "surf the web," "iron out the wrinkles" in a speech, or "mine" data, you are speaking metaphorically. On any day that you "score a home run" in business, sell a "cash cow" product, and "move the needle" on a project, or you find yourself "behind the eight ball," "off your customers' radar screens," and about to "tank," you are speaking metaphorically. If you've "hit the glass ceiling" or are lucky enough to get a "golden parachute," you are speaking metaphorically. Like fish unaware of water because it totally surrounds them, people are often unaware of how readily and constantly they draw comparisons to navigate through the workday.

For one day, stop yourself from using any metaphoric language. Just make simple statements. Instead of saying, "We need to drill down further here," say, "We need to go into greater detail." Instead of saying, "My computer almost crashed today," say, "My computer almost stopped working." See how often you will have to catch yourself. (A variation on this exercise is to keep count of how many metaphors you use in a day or count how many you hear other people using.) If you put away a dollar for each time that you have to stop yourself, you will find yourself with a bundle of dough at the end of the day!

Coming up with vivid metaphors is easier than you think. You are already an unconscious, natural metaphor user.

Rosencrantz: ***What are you playing at?***
Guildenstern: ***Words, words. They're all we have to go on.***

—Tom Stoppard, "Rosencrantz and Guildenstern Are Dead"

YOUR TURN

Now prove it to yourself. The exercises below start easy and get progressively more challenging. By the end of this warm-up, however, you'll be ready to flex your new metaphor muscle in any situation.

1. **See Similarities in Groups:** Metaphor-makers are quick to see similarities between and among different things.

   A. What do each of these sets of words have in common?

   Example: *Red, Blue, Green*
   Answer: *All are colors*

   Calves, Chicks, Puppies ______________________
   Toothpicks, Paper, Cartons ______________________
   Jello, Clay, Minds ______________________

   B. List at least five things that have the quality of each of the following:

   Example: *Things that are red*
   Answer: *Blood, fire engines, blushing faces, stoplights, hearts, Coca-Cola cans, noses in winter, bulls-eyes, the Chinese flag, apples, Santa Claus's outfit, matador's cape, valentine hearts*

   Things that are sweet: ______________________
   Things that smell bad: ______________________
   Activities that are difficult to do: ______________________
   Events that make people smile: ______________________
   Noises that would wake people from sleep: ______________________
   ____

2. **See Dissimilarities:** As important as it is to see similarities, it is equally important to see when thing are not similar so that you don't create a bad metaphor like "as strong as a poodle."

   A. Which word does **not** belong in each group?

   Example: *Burrito, egg roll, blintz, pancake*
   Answer: *Pancake. The others are all rolled foods that hold fillings inside them.*

   New York City, Chicago, Des Moines, Los Angeles ____________
   Frog, snake, deer, elephant______________________
   Golf, tennis, swimming, skiing ______________________

3. Make Simple Comparisons

A. With each of the subjects below, complete the thought, "At that moment, I was **as happy as...**"

Example: *A doctor who has just paid off her last college loan!*

A child who ______________________________
A track star who ______________________________
A scientist who ______________________________
A salesperson who ______________________________

B. An unsolicited email came to me with these metaphors that describe how stupid someone might be
—All foam, no beer
—His antenna are not picking up all channels
—His chimney's clogged
—His elevator doesn't go up to the top floor
—She is a few clowns short of a circus
—Her receiver is off the hook
—There's no grain in the silo

What metaphors can you create from these other categories that **capture the idea** of "stupid"?

Cooking ______________________________
Automobiles ______________________________
Medicine ______________________________
Ice skating ______________________________

4. See Analogous Relationships

A. In each pair of words below there is a specific relationship. Select the set of words below that pair with the same relationship. Read the words this way: Mother is to Daughter as ______ is to ______

Example:
Mother : Daughter? (Same sex parent is to child as...)

Mother : Son?
Yes, she is the parent to both, but the similarity of gender is missing

Mother : Father?
They are related, but not the same way

Mother : Niece?
Same gender, but wrong relationship

Father : Son?
Same relationship and same gender – right choice

Hammer : Carpenter
Chalk : Teacher
Knowledge : Librarian
Patients : Doctor
Laboratory : Scientist

Professor : Scholarly
Lawyer : Litigation
Hero : Brave
Man : Handsome
Nurse : Doctor

Pray : Church
Dream : Sleep
Drink : Glass
Act : Stage
Write : Book

B. If your company were an insect or animal, what would it be? Why? If your competition were an insect or animal, what would it be? Why?

Example:

My company would be a bumble bee. Aerodynamically, bees shouldn't be able to fly, but they do. Given our small company size, we shouldn't be able to deliver the volume of quality work we produce, but we do!

The competition would be a turtle. They are slow and steady, but cannot move quickly when circumstances call for it.

My company would be a ____________________
because ____________________

My competition would be a____________________
because ____________________

C. Who is this **person** like? Select a friend, a relative, and a colleague and describe them using only the names of other well-known people, or characters. Aim for at least three well-known people or characters. Then, bullet point **why** you chose those characters.

Example:

My friend Nancy is a combination of Martha Stewart, Einstein, and Seinfeld. She is:
—creative with decorating
—smart as can be at work, and
—can talk about nothing, socially, for hours!

My friend ______________ is a combination of ___________
He/she is ______________________________________

My relative______________ is a combination of ___________
He/she is ______________________________________

My colleague______________ is a combination of ___________
He/she is ______________________________________

D. What is your **city** like? Aim for at least three different answers.

My city is like(a) ______________________________
because ____

My city is like(a) ______________________________
because ____

My city is like(a) ______________________________
because ____

"My favorite city in the world is New York. Sure, it's dirty—but like a beautiful woman smoking a cigar."

—Joan Rivers

E. If your company were a **color,** what color would it be? **Why?** What would your competition's color be? **Why?**

Example:

It would be forest green, because we are a very sophisticated, but understated consulting firm. We don't advertise. We don't do public relations. Our comprehensive analyses customized to each client and our professional implementation earn us additional work.

Our competition is brown, the color of cooked cookie dough, because they do cookie-cutter work. They have one solution

for every problem and their implementation always follows the same path.

What would be a good color for your company?______________
Why? ____

What would be a good color for your competition? __________
Why? ____

Pick Up the Pace

1. Look at the figure below.

What do you see? A black dot on a white page? How about a polar bear's nose in a snowstorm? The black eye of a witch? A raisin floating in milk?

When you were a child, you probably would have seen all these things and more. That imaginative childhood ability to "see" possibilities everywhere is a critical part of metaphorical thinking and selling. We all have that ability. It just has to be teased out of us. Try these exercises.

A. List **5 things** you can do or make with bricks. (e.g., Doorstop. Build a well.)

B. How many words with three or more letters can you make with these letters? R G K I G S I F N

C. What **images** would you use to represent each of the following feelings or concepts? Try for three each.

Example: *Freedom*
—the American flag
—a person breaking the chains that bind him
—a bird flying out of its cage

Frustration ______________________________________
Love ____
Relief ____

2. The pairs of words below are initially unrelated. Yet, with a little similarity/comparison thinking, you will be able to make parallel connections. ____________________

Example: *How are an iceberg and a good idea related?*

Answers: ***Both can be big. Both can be broken down into smaller chunks. If they're good, they are solid. Often you see the tip of both first, but the deeper down you go into them, the larger they become. Icebergs move. Ideas can move from one department to another.***

How can the following be related?

1. A rose and a salesperson
2. Riding a bike and a difficult client
3. A balloon and our government

Answers:
See Similarities: All are babies. All are made from wood. All can be molded.
See Dissimilarities: Des Moines is not a major US city. Snake (only one that slithers to move), swimming (only one that does not need special equipment to hold while doing).
See analogous relationship: A. Chalk : Teacher. Chalk is a teacher's tool. B. Hero : Brave. The adjective is a quality usually associated with the noun. C. Act : Stage. You may dream in your sleep, but sleep is not a place.
Pick Up the Pace Brick/s: Uses limited only by your imagination. Some uses: build a house, edge a garden, book-ends, weapon, crush them and make a gravel path, work-out weights, paint them and create a work of art. Letters: Frisking, risking, skiing, frisk, risk, rink, ring, sink, king, grin, skin, skin, sin, gin, kin, sir, fir, ink.

Chapter 3

When Do You Need Metaphors?

WHICH OF THESE QUESTIONS are most challenging for you to address when you are selling your particular product, service or idea?

1. *Who are you?*
2. *What do you do?*
3. *How do you do it?*
4. *Why does what you do or advocate matter?*
5. *How are you different?*
6. *Why do I need you?*
7. *Whom else have you worked with?*
8. *How long will this take?*
9. *How much will it cost?*
10. *Why should I do this now?*

These are your likely metaphor moments.

You know you're going to need a metaphor if at any time during your sales call or presentation you expect to encounter one of these

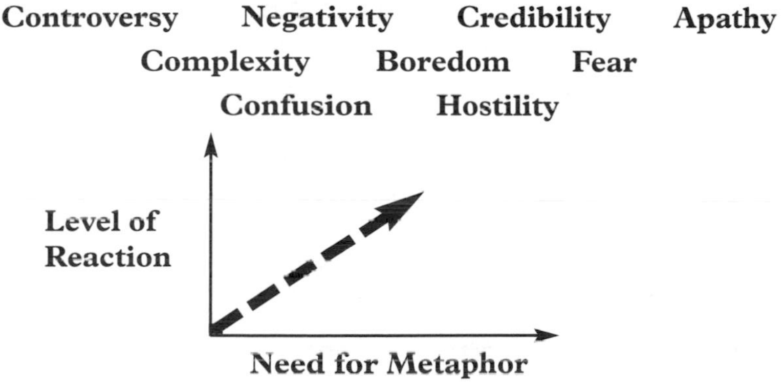

reactions. And, as the chart indicates, the stronger the expected reaction, the more your argument needs metaphor.

Anticipate where you're likely to encounter these reactions—and why—so you can prepare accordingly. For instance, your client may be hostile to the suggestion of scheduling an initial meeting. Once you've got your foot in the door, he may become bored or confused by your explanations. At the end of your presentation, he may be unwilling to allocate the funds or manpower. Or he may be reluctant to hire you because he perceives no urgency. By anticipating resistance, you can actually head it off with a metaphor you've thought out beforehand. The best offense may in fact be a good defense.

Just remember, when you're up against a fortress of resistance, that lobbing more facts and figures at your client won't get your message across. Metaphors help by either 1) warding off the resistance altogether, shifting your listener out of his defensive mindset or shedding light on his confusion so that he is open to what you're proposing, or 2) disarming him after he's hurled objections at you.

A Most Unusual Metaphor Moment

Prostitutes in India, often the sole breadwinners for their families, are very afraid of contracting AIDS yet do not wish to displease their madams. They have embarked on a campaign to get their madams to insist that customers use condoms. What is the selling argument? As reported in *The New York Times,* "Delegations of prostitutes visit madams and tell them, 'If you want to enjoy the fruits of the tree, you must keep the tree healthy.'"[1]

Not every sales situation will require metaphor; you may find yourself seeing eye-to-eye from the minute you introduce yourself to the moment you offer up a contract for signature. But a good practitioner is always prepared for emergencies, ready to apply powerful metaphors when communication starts to fail. In a sales-threatening emergency—and they happen to even the best-prepared presenters—metaphors are like Type O blood: If you've got a supply on hand, you can handle any hemorrhage. At any time you sense your client or audience slipping away from you—on the phone, around a table, in a large conference setting—administer a quick infusion of imagery, and you'll see life and color return.

And then you'll find your client of a mind to reward you with his business and support.

Chapter 4

Your Audience's Brain Craves *Metaphors*

METAPHORS, I'VE CLAIMED, CAN be heard over the static buzz of too many words. They penetrate your client's innate defenses; they shed light on his confusion; they cause a shift in his perceptions; they move him to action.

But why? Why do images hit the mark and stick better than words? Why do feelings register better than facts? *Why metaphor?*

To understand why metaphors win you sales, you must first better understand how your client's brain works. The brain is not, as it appears, just a single mass of gray matter: It has two distinct hemispheres, Left Brain and Right, each highly specialized in function. Both are packed with neurons capable of sorting out the torrent of stimuli you work your way through every day.

The two hemispheres are linked by a dense membrane of nerve conduits called the corpus callosum. Though both sides of the brain are always in communication, they're receptive to different kinds of information. In the late '60s and early '70s, Roger Sperry at The California Institute of Technology did experiments with a neurologically impaired person whose corpus callosum was severed. When statistics and facts were presented to this person, the left side of the brain showed electrical activity and the right side was quiet. When the researchers told a story, the right side fired up while the left side continued with reduced electrical activity.

Now consider what this says about your client. The left side of his brain fires when you present him with facts, e.g., a spreadsheet with all its data points, or a summary page of attributes, or a statistical break-down of select trends. But on the right side of his brain, *nothing is happening.*

Everyone who sells knows that "a committee buy is a committee sell." You have to meet and satisfy everyone on the committee to get the business. Since people on committees usually have different agendas, you must address all of them or risk losing the sale. You can't afford to get through to only one member of the committee.

Your client is no different. Sitting on his decision-making committee are his two hemispheres, whom I shall dub Joe "Left-Brain" Friday and Robin "Right-Brain" Williams. Joe Left Brain and Robin Right Brain may share the same skull but they have little in common. They work together, but they have decidedly different agendas. To get your client to say yes, you need to speak to and satisfy both of these taskmasters.

At its simplest, Joe LB processes language and data and responds to details, precision, logic, and linear organization. Robin RB processes images and emotions and responds to pictures, humor, color, and novelty. They share what they take in and process: Electronic messages fly back and forth between their offices thanks to the corpus callosum, whose 80 million axons act as a server. (And you think you get a lot of e-mail!)

Why Joe Friday and Robin Williams?

Joe Friday is a famous fictional detective from a program called *Dragnet,* which began on radio, became a very popular TV show in the '50s, and has recently found new life on ABC-TV. Joe was never a flashy kind of guy. His looks are average. His dress is predictable and he likes things all neat and by the book. He is a stickler for details and, through steady perseverance, always gets his man (or woman). In fact, when he is investigating a crime, no matter how distraught the person is he's talking to, he is known for his deadpan delivery of this famous line: "Just the facts, ma'am. Just the facts."

Joe is the cognitive side of your client's brain. He processes language (reading and writing), numbers, sequences, and analyses. Joe loves facts, details, lists, and categories. He thinks analytically, reductively, objectively. He works like a calculator, or a word processor. Joe Left Brain is the one who makes it possible for us to make our to-do lists, work out our taxes, plan account strategies, schedule the week, speak, figure out how to put together that some-assembly-required piece of furniture for the playroom, learn a new language, decide on a mortgage, and list the pluses and minuses of taking that new job.

In selling, when you say:

- *There are three reasons why this makes sense. First…Second…Third…*
- *The system works this way…*
- *Our timetable lays out this way…*
- *Program A is for Human Resources. Program B is for Marketing.*
- *We can do this under budget and within one week of the deadline.*
- *Bottom-line, this will increase productivity by 20 percent.*

Joe Left Brain is very happy!

Robin Williams probably needs less of an introduction. He is the wacky, spontaneous, intuitive, imaginative, childlike, playful, emotional, creative comedian/actor we all know from movies such as "Mrs. Doubtfire," "Good Morning, Vietnam," "Dead Poet's Society," and "Bird Cage;" and as the voice of the genie in "Aladdin;" and from his outrageous HBO stand-up acts.

Robin Williams is the nonverbal side of your client's brain. Robin Right Brain specializes in images, spatial relationships, rhythm, music, emotion, and color. Robin is intuitive, impressionistic, and symbolic; he sees the big picture, recognizes patterns, and makes connections. Robin "reads" people well by noticing body language and tone of voice. He processes like a food blender, arriving at his end product by throwing everything into the mix.

Robin Right Brain enables us to daydream, decorate a room, finger-paint, listen to music, laugh at a joke, recognize faces of people, groove to reggae, get lost in the latest John Grisham novel, cry for the astronauts lost in the space shuttle *Columbia,* frolic in the snow, and imagine the lives we want for our children or our companies.

In selling, when we:

- show visuals
- demonstrate an action or process
- play a video
- use metaphors and analogies
- tell a joke
- deviate from the script

Robin Right Brain is very happy!

The "Committee"

Joe Left Brain	**Robin Right Brain**
Language	Emotion
Logic	Images
Categories	Patterns
Linear thinking	Creative thinking
Numbers	Music
Details	Rhythm
Analysis	Synthesis

It's hard to imagine two characters with less in common. Can you see them being pals, going out for a beer together, or wanting to spend any time with each other?

Yet they work together rather well. When you say, "I don't have a good feeling about this," that is Robin Right Brain talking. When you say, "I think this is the best way to go for these three reasons," that is Joe Left Brain speaking up. And when you say, "Not only does this add up on paper, but my gut tells me to go ahead," that is Joe and Robin working together for you.

Joe and Robin together take in the tide of information the eyes, ears, nose, tongue, and skin are collecting, then sort it, make sense of it, and act sensibly on it. However, like executives who would get nothing done if they took every phone call, read every piece of mail, and saw everyone who wanted an appointment with them, Joe and Robin are selective about what they pay attention to. With 100 billion neurons each making an average of 1,000 connections for some 100 trillion interconnections, they cannot afford to prioritize everything. They grab onto information—and this is key—*when it strikes a meaningful chord.* The rest they ignore or quickly forget.

Confronted with emotionally charged input, the human brain actually becomes more efficient at thinking (unless the input is of a traumatizing nature, which may leave us momentarily speechless). That's because emotions produce endorphins, chemical messengers which increase the flow of neurotransmitters that allow brain cells to communicate. In plain English, if Robin is made to *see and feel* something—to experience either the aha! of recognition or the wow! of the unexpected—Joe can prioritize and process data better.

Likewise, your client will not hear and retain your plea over every other request for his attention that day *unless it resonates with Robin* as well as registers with Joe. The red-hot message you thought you left in the morning cools down considerably by the flood of the day's other incoming messages. You must package your message in verbal color and heightened emotion if you want your client's executive committee—Joe and Robin—to salvage it from the tidal wave of stimuli washing over them every minute.

Tell Joe. Show Robin.

Now try pitching them.

Let's say you're a copywriter for an ad agency, and you've got the National Airlines account. National has just spent a bundle revamping its fleet of aircraft to give passengers a few more inches of leg room. National's clientele is everyone who's ever spent two hours in the air with their knees touching the meal tray in front of them. How do you reach that clientele?

> **Approach A:** *Fly Coach on National. National removed 7500 seats from their entire fleet (over 700 aircraft). They completed this entire reconfiguration in only one month and now provide six and a half more inches in Coach class per seat. The FAA said this was one of the fastest reconfigurations it had ever seen.*
>
> **Approach B:** *Fly Coach on National and cross your legs in comfort.*

For the pitch to succeed, remember, both Joe and Robin must be satisfied. Here's how they process the input:

Joe, the analytical buyer, responds to Approach A. He appreciates all those particulars about the reconfiguration: the number of seats, the speed with which they were installed. To Joe, six and a half inches of additional leg room translates into a buy.

Robin, however, is unmoved by just the facts. To choose the experience National is offering, he's got to see it. Hence Robin responds to Approach B—to the image of having more leg room in coach—because that image triggers a sense of physical relief. He can feel what it's like to cross his legs in comfort.

So which do you choose? Both—with a stronger emphasis on Approach B.

Because, though most people assume Joe rules the roost, Robin actually has the upper hand, the last word, the final vote. Because here's the shocking thing about the Joe/Robin partnership: *They're not really equals.*

Wired for the Visual

The dirty little secret about the human brain is that, despite its phenomenal evolution from little more than an olfactory knob, it's still wired to respond more to the emotional than to the cognitive, more to the visual than to the verbal. As every good copywriter knows, what gets our attention, what sticks in our memory, what moves us is what we are made to see and, consequently, feel. As wonderfully rational as we are, as incredibly computer-like our minds, our brains crave pictures the way a child craves candy.

Joe understands "I love New York," but Robin lights up when he sees "I ♥ New York."

Even Einstein said, "If I can't see it, I don't understand it."

Furthermore, experiments suggest our visual recall is almost limitless. In one, people were shown 2,560 photographic slides at the rate of one every ten seconds. One hour later, they were shown 280 pairs of slides in which one member of each pair was a picture from the original series and the other, though similar, was not. Subjects recognized 80-85% correctly.

Pictures Speak Louder Than Words

The retina of your eye contains 150 million rod and cone cells for detecting changes in light and color. Those receptors send information to the cerebral cortex through two optic nerves, each consisting of 1 one million nerve fibers. Neurons devoted to visual processing number in the hundreds of millions and account for 30% of the brain's cortex. By comparison, each of your auditory nerves consists of a mere 30,000 fibers, and the neurons devoted to auditory processing account for only 3% of your cortex.

We process visuals much faster than words. That is one reason why advertisements generally show a picture of the product they are selling in addition to any printed or spoken words that might accompany it. Imagine trying to sell a Porsche, a diamond, or a vacation destination without pictures.

- We remember 20% of what we hear
- We remember 80% of what we hear and see
- **When images are vivid, we remember 95%**

The lesson for salespeople: you have greater selling impact when you use words that create images in your listener's mind.

Wired to Make Associations

If you speak in visuals, you will get Robin's attention. But if you want to drive home a point, you must speak to Robin in visuals *he can relate to.*

The brain "sees" only what it has experienced in some way. For example, if I said to you, "The CEO of the company is like George Jordan," you would neurologically register the words, but you would have no reaction. You'd have no reaction because you'd have no picture. You'd have no picture because you have no experience of a George Jordan.

Even if I passionately repeated that the CEO was like George Jordan, you'd still draw a blank. You'd find me annoying, or tune me out; I'd become background noise. My repeating the name in hopes of communicating with you would be like raising my voice to get through to someone who doesn't speak English.

However, if I said to you, "The CEO was like Michael Jordan," or "like George Bush," unless you've been on the moon for the last several years, you would react neurologically with an explosion of associations, images, and emotions (positive or negative). Michael Jordan is someone Joe Left Brain has filed in his drawer of great basketball players; George Bush is someone Joe reads about every day. Robin Right Brain sees not only each celebrity but conjures up a host of related images: Nike sneakers, "Sports Illustrated" covers, Madison Square Garden, and the like for Michael; the White House, certain headlines, and Iraqi battle scenes for George. Negative or positive, the images come almost unbidden upon hearing the familiar words.

Think how a song from your youth replayed on the radio can suddenly make you ache like a teenager. Think how hearing just the two words, "Nine Eleven," or seeing the numbers "9-11" flood you with pictures of the Twin Towers and emotion-laden memories of what happened on that fateful day. Think how a certain combination of breeze, temperature, and sky color can set off a cavalcade of memories from an earlier time in your life—your wedding day, summer camp, visits to a favorite relative—simply because these sensory inputs match up with those of your own past experience.

Your brain is in fact more like a scrapbook than it is a computer. Each of us represents a unique collection of triumphs and tragedies, joys and disappointments, satisfactions and apprehensions. My memory scrapbook includes growing up in the city in a tiny apartment with my parents and brother, playing ball in the streets, going to the country in the summers, nearly drowning in a lake, always being the tallest girl in the class, being a card shark at age eight, working in libraries, teaching, working on Wall Street, losing my father, falling in love, falling out of love, going on a safari, completing an Outward Bound program, landing on a glacier, collecting art, participating in the Aspen Institute, buying my co-op, watching my niece and nephew grow into wonderful young adults, and, most recently, performing in a cabaret.

Your memory album, it's safe to say, does not consist of these entries. And yet it's also a pretty good bet that we share, if not identical experiences, then some common images. The beach shot of me was taken on a different beach than yours, but we both know what it feels like to be sunburned, and gritty with sand, and tired from swimming against the tide. The trick to making a winning metaphor lies in figuring out which of your client's photos you know something about—enough to trigger an explosion of associations in his mind.

When you present terms, concepts, references, features, benefits, arguments or value propositions that do not call up familiar experiences in the vast scrapbook of your client's mind, your message will not be as strongly understood, appreciated or internalized as it would with the addition of an image. No matter how much passion you display for what's in your scrapbook, you will not arouse similar excitement in your client unless you can relate to his album of photos. A feeling you know as "exhilarating as skiing on new fallen snow" will fall on deaf ears to someone raised on the beaches of Florida. What is personal clicks. What is alien is rejected.

You may be asking, "How do I know what exists in my client's scrapbook?" You know more than you think (I'll prove this to you in Section Two). But here's another little secret about the brain you can use to your advantage when groping for a visual your client can relate to: The brain doesn't necessarily give higher priority to reality. What it can imagine is just as visual—and thus emotionally powerful—as what it has actually experienced. Your brain has no trouble seeing a yellow brick road, though you have never traveled on one. It gets childishly happy at the prospect of a fat man bringing toys made by elves at the North Pole, though no such person exists. It can imagine an elephant in a purple hot air balloon floating over the Atlantic, not because it has actually done that itself, but because it has the previous reference points for floating, purple, elephant, and the Atlantic and can put them together into a new image.

With just a little nudging, in short, the brain can take what it does know to imagine what it doesn't. If I said, "The head of the company is like George Jordan: He's got the energy and talent of Michael Jordan and the personality of George Bush," you would get what I meant. In a flash you would have synthesized two separate and distinct sets of images into something new and yet meaningful.

Therefore, to sell or explain anything new and with impact to someone, you must not merely play to the brain's preference for the visual: You have to seize on those visuals your listener's brain *already understands from experience.* Drawing on photos from its own scrapbook, the brain can synthesize new pictures and derive from them the meaning you intend.

Dr. John Gofman, physician and nuclear chemist, had to testify in the Karen Silkwood trial against Kerr-McGee. The group of ordinary citizens on the jury in Oklahoma City did not understand that infinitesimal amounts of plutonium in the lungs cause lung cancer. Recognizing that they would not be familiar with alpha particles, he used a metaphor to explain how plutonium damages lung cells.

"So, when people say a small amount of this won't hurt you [which Kerr McGee had alleged], that is so absurd one wonders how anyone can think it. *Expecting that an alpha particle will go through a cell and not do horrible damage is like ramming an ice pick through a fine Swiss watch or shooting a machine gun through a television set and saying it will function just fine.*"

The jury found in favor of the Silkwood family.[1]

---

hp demonstrates a perfect committee pitch to Joe and Robin in an ad for super-scalable servers. The ad copy first tells Joe what these servers do:

> *They give you virtually unlimited server capacity by combining instant capacity on demand, mc/serviceguard and virtual partitions.*

The ad states how these servers help:

> *Now you can have instant access to as much server capacity as you need, whenever you need it.*

But then **hp** shifts into high metaphoric gear and the advertising copy speeds right to Robin's joy buzzer:

> *How you'd describe it to a car salesman: It's like a compact car that seats a soccer team, turns into a top-fuel dragster when you're in a hurry and never runs out of gas.*[2]

Wired for the *Unexpected*

1. Which letter is your eye drawn to?
   ooooooooooooooooooooXoooooooooo
2. Which name gets your attention in this list?
   John, Jim, Ken, Sam, David, Dracula, Lou, Ben, Harry
3. Which statement gets your strongest reaction?
   A. I went across town by bus today with my baby.
   B. The baby was crying on the bus.
   C. I left the baby on the bus!
4. If you were browsing the shelves in a bookstore, which books would you pull out to examine?
   A. *Relationships Between Men and Women*
   B. *If You Can't Live Without Me, Why Aren't You Dead Yet?*[2]
5. Which airline safety instruction would make you stop reading your magazine or book?
   A. "Under your seat is a life-jacket. Please remove it if instructed by the crew."
   B. "In the event this flight suddenly becomes a cruise, you'll find your life-jacket under your seat."

Relying on the unexpected is an excellent way to grab Joe and Robin's attention. It's the key to successful marketing, as Seth Godin so ably illustrates in his book, *Purple Cows.* Most products, he says, are like brown cows. On a country drive, you will notice the first brown cow you see on a country drive, but after seeing hundreds of them, they will no longer catch your eye. However, if on the next curve, you see a purple cow, you will absolutely notice it. Godin's message is that companies need to continually introduce "purple cows" to be remarkable to grab their consumer's attention.

Metaphors are *verbal* purple cows. They work by taking the same old thing and catching your attention with a fresh view of it. If I were to talk to you about corporate malfeasance, about how Dennis Kozlowski, the indicted CEO of Tyco International LTD swindled investors out of millions, you would probably...yawn. You've heard it all, or some version of it, before. But if I were to describe another CEO at another company and say, "He spends like Dennis Kozlowski. He's got six-thousand-dollar shower curtains in his budget"—now I've made a purple cow out of a brown one.

Section Summary

When you see clients' eyes glaze over (often on the twentieth slide of bullet points in a PowerPoint presentation), notice them doodling, staring at you with completely blank expressions, or even raising their hands to say, *Enough!* there is a good chance you are spending too much time selling to Joe, the logical decision-maker, and that you are ignoring Robin, his visual and emotional, but senior, partner.

You need to start talking more to Robin because Robin is the key to your sale. When he "sees" what you are saying, relates to it, and becomes emotionally involved with it, he will swing the vote in your favor.

Section Two
Building Metaphor Muscle

"If I were a car, you could find the words."

Chapter 5

The Four-Step Metaphor Workout: Overview

SAY YOU'RE IN A competitive shoot-out for a large piece of business. You have no direct experience in your prospect's industry—and industry experience is your prospect's number-one selection criteria. Furthermore, you are up against the biggest and best-known firms in your field, one of whom specializes in the industry in which you have no prior experience. You have one shot to present your case to the senior vice president, whom, just to make things more interesting, you have never met.

That was exactly my seemingly hopeless situation when I competed for the Presentation Skills training contract of a leading advertising agency in New York.

What would you do? Here's what I did.

Analogy to the Rescue

It took me a few days to come up with the analogy that won me the business, but that thinking time was worth it. In our meeting, when the senior vice president objected to my lack of direct experience with advertising agencies, the conversation went this way:

> ***Me:*** *That is true, but let me ask you a question. You just won the DHL account [I had done my homework]. How much prior experience did your agency need to have in the overnight courier business to have the right to do DHL's advertising? Let me suggest that the answer is "none." You would learn the dynamics of the overnight courier business the way you learned the dynamics of the businesses of your other accounts [which I then named]. DHL just had to be sure you were the best darn advertising agency around. Isn't that true?*
>
> ***SVP:*** *[Drawing the word out slowly] Y-e-e-s…*

Me: *Well, the same is true with me. I don't have to have an ad agency in my portfolio of accounts to do your presentation-skills training. I'll learn the dynamics of your agency quickly the way I have the investment-banking, aerospace, and magazine industries, to name just three. You just have to be sure I know a heck of a lot about presenting—and I do. [Those last three words were said with quiet, rock-solid certainty and laser-lock eye contact.]*

SVP: *[She tilted her head sideways as the analogy sunk in and all she said was a quiet…] Oh.*

My analogy completely changed the way my prospect "saw" her number-one buying criteria (specific industry experience). To deny me my point would have been to deny her agency's right to any business in an industry new to them, clearly an untenable position. Even if her agency had had another overnight courier service account in the past—say, Fedex—my analogy would have still held, because there would have been a first time they won an account in the overnight courier business. It didn't hurt that I was modeling what I was selling, i.e., the ability to persuade, to present a winning argument.

The analogy won me the business. The agency has been my client for over ten years.

Now, how did I come up with such a winning metaphor? I followed a simple four-step model:

Four Steps to a Winning Metaphor

1. Determine the Client's Blindspot
2. Snapshot the Client
3. Create the Comparison
4. Relate

---

1. Determine the Client's Blindspot

My client's blindspot was the agency's insistence on previous industry experience. They couldn't see how someone without previous experience could be nonetheless highly qualified to do the job.

2. Snapshot the Client

I knew the agency's reputation. I knew the job titles of key players. I knew their account list. I knew they did business in New York. I knew they had just won the DHL account.

3. Create the Comparison

I decided to create my analogy on the basis of knowing they had just won the DHL account.

I compared their right to win DHL's business, despite having no prior specific industry experience, to my right to win their business without an ad agency in my portfolio.

4. Relate

I concluded by saying that in a similar fashion to how they work, I was qualified to do the job for them as well.

I related their right to win DHL's business, despite having no prior specific industry experience, to my right to win their business without an ad agency in my portfolio.

Let's examine each step of the model in detail and then apply it to the many phases of a sales call.

Chapter 6

Identify Blindspot

JOEL, THE MARKETING DIRECTOR at a small but successful consumer appliance company, had waited patiently for Richard, SVP of Finance, to return from one of his many overseas vacations to present a new, expanded Customer Relationship Management program to him. Joel had just returned from a CRM conference and was fired up with several ideas from that event that he believed would enhance business for his firm.

Richard listened politely while Joel explained how customers might be better retained. "Nice presentation, Joel," he said finally. "But let me remind you that we put out the best product in the market. We back it up with a full-service guarantee and we offer twenty-four-hour telephone support in case anyone has a problem. I would say we have a very successful customer relations program. I haven't stayed head of finance for ten years by spending any more than we needed to—from paper clips to new office space—and I certainly don't intend to change that practice now."

"True," responded Joel, "but that is my point exactly. This will be as important to our growth as any investment we can make. Customers have become more sophisticated, and in this competitive market we can't take their loyalty for granted. A more robust CRM program will help us sell new products more easily and keep old customers coming back."

Richard shook his head. "Sorry, Joel," replied Richard. "I'm afraid I have to turn down your request for funds."

"But—," sputtered Joel.

Richard held up a hand. "The answer is no. Now, if you'll excuse me, I have to leave for my committee meeting." He rose from his desk and walked out.

Why can't Richard "see" the wisdom of Joel's recommendation? Does he have:

A. A bias against CRM?
B. A lack of funds for an expanded CRM?
C. A lack of faith in Joel's credibility?
D. A lack of understanding of the power of CRM?
E. A fear of loss of control over the current CRM?

The answer is not (A). Richard has nothing against CRM. He is proud of the client relationship program they have in place now. It is not (B)—he never says there is no money in the budget. Nor does he indicate he harbors any doubts about Joel (C) or his own ability to keep a tight rein on costs (E).

The answer is (D). Richard has a conceptual blindspot. The guy just doesn't *see* the advantages of a CRM program beyond what the firm is already doing.

Diagnosis

The first step in overcoming client resistance, his blindspot, is to identify what lies behind it. What is keeping your client or listener from literally seeing what you mean?

There are two kinds of resistance: *objective* and *subjective*. The first kind you can take at face value because it's based on fact. For instance, your client won't go forward because he hears you say you can deliver on the 12th, and he has to have delivery on the 10th. The only way to clear up his resistance is to find a way to deliver on the 10th. Or your client is operating under a simple misconception: He thought your firm was in the business of forging tools when actually you're in the business of packaging and delivering them. Again, you can set him straight rather easily. He's just got the facts wrong.

The second kind of resistance, however—what I call a conceptual blindspot—is not so easily overcome. It's subjective, meaning it has its roots in emotion and won't be dislodged with facts. For example, your client may have had a bad experience with a product similar to yours and he cannot shake his conviction that all such products are profoundly flawed. His skepticism won't be pushed aside by yet another explanation; it isn't based on reason.

You need him to see your product in a whole new way, one which doesn't summon any of his resistance. You need to transport him from that place where he has dug in his heels to a whole new place, where he cannot bring his emotional baggage. You need to make your appeal to his right brain, in the *right-brain language of metaphor,* because that's where subjective resistance takes root and burrows deep.

But first you must listen to him with your right brain. You must hear what he's probably not saying, not in so many words. (We have an expression for this: "Read between the lines.") It's easier than you think; in the examples below, you'll find that you're already familiar with the most typical forms of emotional resistance.

Classic Blindspots

Dennis, a retired insurance sales person, told me about a client of his, Carl, a young pediatrician, who just wouldn't sign the necessary papers to put the insurance in place that he said he wanted for his family. Dennis couldn't understand the delay, because Carl had seemed very happy with the coverage Dennis proposed. When pressed, Carl simply said, "Yes, I know this is important, but it's no longer at the top of my priority list at this moment. My nurse just quit, my youngest is having problems in school, and, to top it off, my apple trees seem to have suddenly developed some sort of blight. Besides, my wife and I are only thirty-two and our kids are only five and seven. We are all basically healthy. This can wait."

What is Carl's *real* objection? Is it that:

A. Carl feels he and his family don't really need insurance?
B. Protection right now doesn't seem critical?
C. Carl's funds are going to other priorities?

It certainly isn't (A); it was Carl who initiated the sale. Nor is it (C). Carl never said he was having trouble financing the insurance. The answer is (B). Because of unexpected recent events, *Carl sees no urgency to take action.* And until Dennis perceives Carl's blindspot, he won't get the papers signed—and may even lose the sale by repeatedly pressing his client for them.

Linda R., an account manager for *Today's Woman* magazine, was pitching her title to Nick, the media planner at Monster Advertising Agency. The day she arrived for her appointment, Nick's office looked like a tornado had just ripped through it. Media kits lay piled and strewn on the floor. Nick's desk had so many magazines and papers on it that the picture of an attractive young woman barely peeked through the mess. Nick himself seemed highly distracted. He fidgeted a great deal during her presentation.

"Let me be honest with you," he said, as she concluded. "Your book is not likely to be on the list. There isn't enough money in the budget to add it to the five titles I've already got."

Linda heard what Nick said, but couldn't pinpoint the resistance behind it. "You want to maximize your budget, Nick. Can you tell me why my publication would not help you do that?"

"Look, there are ten titles in this category, all of them women's magazines, all of them targeted to readers between eighteen and thirty-four," he responded. "We've selected five for their reach to our target market. Your book doesn't make the cut." He shrugged. "Sorry. Maybe next time."

What is Nick's blindspot here? Is it that he:

A. Doesn't think her publication is as good as the others?
B. Considers space in her magazine too expensive?
C. Sees no difference between her magazine and the others?

It isn't (A). The quality of her publication was never questioned. Budget is a factor, but there is money for five books, so budget alone does not explain why Linda's publication wouldn't be among the five chosen. The answer is (C). Nick doesn't perceive any differences among the magazines in Linda's category. He believes it doesn't matter which of them he picks, provided they have the numbers to show they reach his target market.

Linda will need a metaphor that shatters that perception. Her publication is not a commodity. She must make Nick "see" *uniqueness among apparently identical choices.*

What you may hear a client tell you is one thing; what you must understand to be his true blindspot is quite another. Here are a few more typical blindspots masquerading as objections:

Objections	**Likely Blindspot**
"You are too expensive."	*Confusing value with price*
"We've always done it this way."	*Fear of change*

"We'll just start with a test."	*Fear of large commitment*
"We're happy with who we have now."	*No perceived value-added*
"Yes—but not now."	*No sense of urgency*
"We've been down that road before."	*Fear of getting burned again*

Summary

- The first step to changing someone's mind is to **identify** the exact nature of his **blindspot**.
- Objective resistance—a simple misunderstanding, or a real problem—can be cleared up with facts or further explanation.
- Subjective resistance, however, is based on emotion or skewed perceptions and will not respond to fact. It is your client's conceptual blindspot, what he cannot or will not see, no matter how much factual explanation you offer.

YOUR TURN

Think of a client you're having a tough time winning. What objections, if any, has he voiced?

____

____

____

Which of these objections can you take at face value and clear up with a simple explanation or compromise?

____

____

____

Which one is hiding a subtext—a skewed perception based on emotion or experience or strongly held belief?

____

____

____

Chapter 7

Snapshot Your Client

I ONCE HEARD A FEMALE motivational speaker talk about success in the business world. She was organized. She was passionate. She peppered her speech with vivid baseball and football metaphors, including quotes from football coach Vince Lombardi

And she bombed. Her audience was 100 percent women who didn't relate to a single metaphor she used and tuned her out.

Know Your Client

The number one rule in selling is to put your client in the center of any communication. What you know about your client is as important, if not more so, than what it is you want to say. The same principle holds true in the creation of a winning metaphor: for it to work, it must draw on images and emotions from your client's world.

My motivational speaker violated that basic principle. She committed the cardinal sales error: she engaged mouth before mind. She didn't take a snapshot of her audience beforehand. If she had, she would have seen that women in business would be alienated by references to the male-dominated world of sports. Many women play sports, but sports do not usually play as central a role in their lives as it does for men. If my speaker was nevertheless determined to use sports analogies, why didn't she profile female athletes? Little as she knew about her listeners, she knew enough to have drawn on more pertinent material for her metaphors.

It's critical that you, too, take a snapshot of your clients before groping for the right metaphor to sway them. What visual images and reference points are in their mental album that you can seize on?

If you were ever presenting to the Ait Hadiddou, a major tribe of Berber people in Morocco, you would be making a major mistake if, in comparing your product's acceptance to falling in love, you said, "This product will capture your heart." The correct metaphor would be, "This product will capture your liver." Among the Ait Hadiddou, the liver is considered the site of true love, not the heart, because it is perceived as the more vital important organ for good health and longevity.

You may be thinking: *But I have no idea what's in his mental album, particularly on an initial sales call. How can I know the first thing about a person I've never met?*

Ah, but you do know—more than you think.

Let's re-visit Joel, Dennis, and Linda, each of whom had to save a sale from a client whose initial response was a flat-out *No.* What do they know? What do they have to work with?

The CRM sale: Joel actually knows a number of things about Richard, having worked under him for years. Richard is 48, married, the father of two, and an ex-marine. Clearly he's a law-and-order man, particular about details, careful with his resources and those of the company. As evidenced by his tenure at the firm, loyalty is a virtue he prizes. He's a financial type, so he reads *The Wall Street Journal* and he votes Republican. Joe happens to know he follows the NASCAR racing circuit. And of course, Richard is fond of travel, especially to remote corners of the globe.

As we'll see in the next chapter, Joel decides to use Richard's love of travel as the basis for the metaphor that would change Richard's view of CRM.

The insurance sale: Dennis's snapshot of Carl is less detailed. He knows his client is a doctor by profession, young, married, with two small children, and a new practice. Carl mentioned during their initial consultation that he had a small-town childhood in the mid-West. He loves to grow things; he has a small orchard on his property.

Dennis decides to use Carl's passion for his apple trees as the basis for the metaphor that will change Carl's sense of urgency about the insurance papers.

The magazine selection sale: Linda's snapshot of Nick is sketchy, since she had only met him this once and, pressed for time, had no chance for the usual small-talk. But she could see by meeting him—the way he was dressed, the style of his glasses, the way he spoke—that he was a typical Gen- X'er, ambitious and overworked, with no time to read all the publications being pitched to him. The photo on his desk was of a woman his age; a fiancée, perhaps, since Nick wore no wedding ring.

Linda decided to select her metaphor from the advertising agency industry—work being Nick's consuming focus—to get Nick to reconsider her publication for his recommended list.

Summary

- The briefest of encounters can supply you with the snapshot you need to create an appropriate metaphor for your sale. Even when you're denied a face-to-face meeting, you always know **something** about a prospective client and his world to create metaphors that will be meaningful to him.
- Snapshot prospects by drawing on their
  - ☐ personal background
  - ☐ industry or business
  - ☐ common knowledge
  - ☐ general life experiences

YOUR TURN

Think of three clients: one whom you know fairly well, one whom you've spoken to or met only once, and one whom you have yet to contact.

1. Name of client I know well ______________________
2. Name of client I only recently met ______________________
3. Name of client I'm going to contact ______________________

Use the categories below to create a snapshot of each.

- **Personal Knowledge:** Male/female? Gen-X'er? Yuppie? Boomer? Senior citizen? Married? Single? Family? Where does client live? Where did client grow up? Where has client lived? Education? Interests? Passions? Sports? Hobbies? What does client read? What is client proud of? Serious/light-hearted temperament? Conservative/Progressive? Risk-taker? Follower/Leader? How is the client dressed? What's in the client's office?

- **Business:** Position? Industry? Past jobs? Past industries? Dynamics of client's business? Achievements? Failures? Clients? Share price? Company growing/shrinking? Industry leader or upstart?
- **Common Knowledge:** Events in the news today affecting client and/or his business? Cultural news—movies, television shows, performances? Current events in sports, the economy, the world?
- **Life Experiences:** The weather? Rush-hour traffic? Raising children? Dieting? Exercise? Home improvement? Computer problems? Programming a VCR? Car trouble? Vacation experiences?

Chapter 8

Create Your Metaphor

JOEL, OUR FRUSTRATED APPLIANCE executive, requested another appointment with Richard, who grudgingly granted it to him. As Joel walked in, Richard quickly reminded Joel that he really wasn't interested in expanding their CRM program.

"Richard, I know that. Let me ask you a question. You are planning a trip to China next year, right?"

"Yes," said Richard warily.

"Which of the following two travel agents would you like to deal with?" Joel took a seat and relaxed into it.

"The first, call her Georgia, listens to where you would like to go, makes the arrangements, books your hotel and drivers, and sends you your ticket. On the trip, everything goes just as planned.

"The second, call her Cathy, handles your trip a little differently. She sends you two itineraries, the one you originally requested and another, slightly different, that reflects your interests. You like the second one much better and book that. Along with your final information and ticket, she sends you reading suggestions, two fiction and two non-fiction, to give you a better feel for Chinese culture, geography, and history. You read one on the plane, and get even more excited about your trip. When you arrive in your hotel, after your very long, tiring trip from the States, there is a Welcome Basket in your room with fresh fruit and bottled sparkling water and a note from Cathy that says, *Enjoy your trip!* And you do. You get to see things and visit places you would never have experienced otherwise, thanks to her thoughtful pre-trip suggestions. When you return home, there is a letter from her welcoming you back. A week later, after jet lag has passed, she calls to hear about what you enjoyed most about your trip. Over the next year, she sends you news about China and other destinations that would appeal to you.

"So which agent would you go with?" Joel concluded.

"The second, of course," replied Richard.

"Yes," said Joel, "because she extended herself to make your trip even more memorable than you could have expected." Richard nodded in agreement. "And it would be fair to say that you would recommend this second agent, yes?" Richard nodded again. "Exactly," triumphed Joel, "because the experience you had with the second was so much richer, more personal, and more satisfying.

"That's what CRM is like," Joel said. "Like Cathy, the travel agent, it generates an experience for the consumer that goes way beyond the product or service being rendered. With CRM, our customers wouldn't be just satisfied with us; they'd be thrilled. They'd go out of their way to recommend us to others."

"I see what you mean," admitted Richard, smiling. "But how expensive will it be?"

"Not as expensive as it will be if we *don't* do it," said Joel. "Let me show you how CRM will pay for itself and grow our customer base…"

Why did this metaphor work? Joel did his homework, which is to say he took what he knew about Richard and created a metaphor that would speak specifically to Richard's right-brain decision-maker. Robin Right Brain related to the travel agent story, being such an experienced traveler himself. From there, it was easy to see how CRM could better manage the customer experience and ultimately increase revenues.

Joel's analogy moved Richard from believing "we don't need it" to "Mmmm, maybe we should talk more about this CRM investment."

If you wish to persuade me, you must speak my words, think my thoughts, and feel my feelings.

—Cicero

Let's explore one more example of a seller who succeeded in removing a client's blindspot by 1) determining the nature of the resistance, 2) taking a snapshot of the client, 3) creating a metaphor based on that snapshot.

Insurance Is to Catastrophe as…

You'll recall that our insurance salesperson Dennis wanted Carl to sign papers to put his insurance policy in place. Dennis had identified Carl's blindspot as a lack of urgency based on a false sense of security because of his youth and current good health. From his snapshot of Carl, Dennis decided he was most comfortable using Carl's love for his orchard as the basis for a winning metaphor.

One Sunday, Dennis showed up at Carl's home unannounced to find Carl spraying his apple trees. "Be right with you," Carl yelled. Dennis waved and walked to the fence where Carl would finish up.

"This orchard must take a lot of tending," said Dennis as Carl moved around the last tree.

"You got that right," replied Carl. "There's always something to deal with, something out of the blue. We'll have a drought, which makes the fruit small and mealy. Or we'll have so much rain, rot sets in. Disease breaks out, or bugs appear. I know the trees look good right now, but if I don't stay on top of this—," Carl nodded at his sprayer—"I could lose the whole lot."

"That's true in my business as well," said Dennis, leaning on a fence post. "People think that because they're healthy right now, they'll always be. They just don't see the need to take preventive measures today, before an unexpected blight strikes tomorrow."

Carl put down his sprayer. "You're talking about those insurance papers, right?"

Dennis nodded. "You and your wife and kids are young and healthy, but—as you so well know, being a doctor—debilitating illness can strike at any time. *Buying insurance today is like treating your apples before blight or insect damage wipes them out. You really can't afford to wait and see what the season will bring.*"

Carl laughed. "I do see your point, Dennis. I suppose you just happen to have the papers with you?"

"But of course," said Dennis, pulling them from his briefcase with a pen for Carl to sign.

Summary

- Create a metaphor based on a detail from your snapshot that will **change the lens** through which your client is seeing your pitch.
- Ask yourself what is this like in my client's life? What else? What else? And, still, what else?

YOUR TURN

From the snapshots you created for three clients in the last chapter, select one item as the basis for a metaphor or analogy that will dissolve the resistance you've met or expect to meet. Now create the analogy or metaphor for these three clients:

1. Client I know well: ____________________

   Key detail from snapshot ____________________

   Metaphor ____________________

2. Client I've met or spoken to once: ____________________

   Key detail from snapshot ____________________

   Metaphor ____________________

3. Client I have yet to meet or speak to: ____________________

   Key detail from snapshot ____________________

   Metaphor ____________________

Chapter 9

Relate Back to Your Point

SOMETIMES, AS WITH CARL in the previous chapter, your client will see where you're going without you having to relate your metaphor back to the situation at hand. But it's important you never assume your client sees the parallel so completely that you needn't underscore it for him. Dennis knew Carl understood the metaphor, and yet he drove home his point by relating it back to insurance: *Buying insurance today is like treating your apples before blight or insect damage wipes them out. You really can't afford to wait and see what the season will bring.*

Linda, our account manager for *Today's Woman,* persisted with Nick, the media buyer, by seizing on what she knew about the advertising industry—specifically, what she knew about Nick's competition.

"Nick, you know the ad agency world," she said. "Would you say Monster—your agency—is the same as competitor Gigundo agency?"

"Of course not," said Nick, leaning forward. "Ours offers a much more integrated approach to our clients. We offer best of breed in all communications from PR to the internet to traditional broadcast and print."

"And Gigundo is more just a holding company for a group of highly independent agencies. Right?" Linda added. Nick nodded.

Linda continued. "Monster and Gigundo are both in the same category—advertising—but with very different features and benefits. Well, the same is true with the women's publication field. All serve the women's market, but offer very different features and benefits to their readers, which is important for advertisers to understand in placing their ads. Let me show you how *Today's Woman* is, in fact, quite different from several of the titles on your list and why it merits being recommended..." Nick lowered his guard and listened.

Why did this analogy ultimately net her the sale? Because Linda not only created an analogy Nick could relate to—she related it back to her own selling point.

Imagine if she had said, "Both advertising agencies are in the same category, but each offers its clients very different features and benefits. Now, let me tell you about *Today's Woman.*" Nick's logical left brain would be saying, *Huh?* Linda was careful to make her analogy complete and parallel. She sketched the advertising world in a way Nick could agree to before relating it to the women's publication world. That linking statement—"the same is true with the women's publication field"—was critical in helping her client move from eye-opening to deal-closing.

Summary

Relating your metaphor or analogy to the topic at hand drives home your point and spares your listener any confusion which might derail the deal.

YOUR TURN

Make sure the metaphors you chose for your three clients in the previous chapter relate back to the point you hope to make with them. If you haven't already related it back to the point you are making to your client, complete that connection now.

Chapter 10

Beware Bad Metaphors!

HOW WOULD YOU COMPLETE this sentence: *People would no sooner give up their cell phones and PCs than give up their __________?*

A top hedge-fund manager, eager to show his audience just how reliant we had all become on technology, completed it this way: "People would no sooner give up their cell phones and PCs than they would give up their toilets." [1]

Toilets?

I doubt that was your choice; had this hedge-fund manager thought about it, he too would have chosen to complete the metaphor differently, because on many levels it simply doesn't work.

First, it's apples to oranges in terms of technology: electronic chip and solid-state circuitry to a water tank with a simple lever and float. Second, a cell phone is an invention of communication. It increases our efficiency by offering access to colleagues, friends, and family anytime, anywhere; it offers us connection when we need it most (such as calling 911 on the highway). I suppose you could argue a toilet, like a cell phone, is an invention of convenience (compared, say, to an outhouse), but it is definitely not something that connects people quickly. The metaphor also fails on an associative level. What we associate with toilets is not what we associate or even want to associate with our cell phones. The word toilet takes us into the bathroom, hardly an appropriate place to shift our thoughts. How much better if the hedge-fund manager had seized upon the world of cars for his metaphor!

Metaphors are like railroad tracks coming from opposite directions to meet in the middle: Each half must wind up close enough to connect, or your argument will derail. Metaphor accidents occur when the visual symbols are mixed, inaccurate, or inappropriate, or when the comparison just isn't completed.

Washing with Tar?

A mixed metaphor brings together too many comparisons to make a point and as a result loses the point in confusion. In the wake of conflict-of-interest scandals, former Chairman of the SEC, Arthur Levitt said, "They're all in the same bathtub and will be tarred with the same brush."[2]

You have to wonder what kind of bubble bath the securities firms are using since we don't usually associate tar with bathing.

Mr. Speaker, I smell a rat! I see it floating in the air; and if it is not nipped in the bud, it will burst forth into a terrible conflagration that will deluge the world![3]

—Sir Boyle Rocher, Irish politician

Close, But Not a Cigar

An inaccurate metaphor brings together two or more factors that just don't make sense. "The boat floated gently across the pond like a slowly thrown bowling ball going down the alley."

Robin Right Brain may be able to see the boat drifting across the pond as well as a bowling ball rolling slowly down an alley, but Joe Left Brain cannot yoke those two images together. A bowling ball just doesn't float. It may meander, but it doesn't bob up and down on an alley of solid oak.

George W. Bush's "axis of evil" phrase describing Iraq, Iran, and North Korea, will go down in history as one of the most inaccurate metaphors ever uttered by a world leader, although it played well in the U.S. The "axis" word was meant to conjure up the negative associations from WW II's Japan, Germany and Italy alliance. The "evil" word was meant to evoke a moral judgment and/or Cold War Russia, which President Reagan had dubbed "The Evil Empire."

While it has a certain rhetorical ring to it, without getting into politics, the metaphor itself just doesn't work. Iraq, Iran, and North Korea are not allies, nor do they have very much in common other than being anti-American dictatorships. The largest war that either Iraq or Iran has fought has been with each other; North Korea is a loner country.[4]

In the 1988 Vice Presidential Debates, the young, then-Senator Dan Quayle attempted to position himself in the minds of viewers in the same category as the enormously popular President Kennedy. He claimed he had as much experience in Congress as John Kennedy did when he sought the presidency. Quayle's opponent, Senator Lloyd Bentsen, skewered him by responding, "Senator, I knew Jack Kennedy. He was a friend of mine. *You*, sir, are no Jack Kennedy."

In one of my seminars, an overzealous young woman thought she was making her point when she said, "When you're on the 100-yard line and things are tense..." Since there is no 100-yard-line in football, this analogy instantly became a fumble.

The Unfinished Symphony

Sometimes a metaphor will fail because it isn't given enough explanation to succeed. Here are some examples:

Incomplete:

Trying to assess the true importance and function of the Net now is like asking the Wright brothers at Kitty Hawk if they were aware of the potential of Frequent Flyer Miles.

Complete:

Trying to assess the true importance and function of the Net now is like asking the Wright brothers at Kitty Hawk if they were aware of the potential of Frequent Flyer Miles. We're always very bad at predicting how a given technology will be used and for what reasons.[5]

Incomplete:

This continuous downsizing is corporate anorexia.

Complete:

This continuous downsizing—it's corporate anorexia. You can get thin, but it's no way to get healthy.[6]

Incomplete:

(National tests) will not help students at all. For example: Does a car go faster when you put another speedometer on it?

Complete:

(National tests) will not help students at all. For example: Does a car go faster when you put another speedometer on it? Obviously, no. You're just measuring the speed again. And when we take a test, it measures our knowledge on that subject, but it won't help us get more knowledge.[7]

What About Clichés?

A cliché, or a faded metaphor, is one that has been so overused it has lost whatever original impact it had to surprise and engage. How many times have you heard:

"We may not hit home runs, but we win by hitting singles and doubles."

"It's apples and oranges."
"A bird in the hand is worth two in the bush."
"We are the Tiffany of the industry."
"It's a jungle out there."
"He's a diamond in the rough"
"The window of opportunity is closing."

Ideally, when you create a metaphor, it's a fresh one—original and specific. However, even a cliché is better than no metaphor at all because it still creates a picture in Robin's right brain. This observation below about paying for seniors' healthcare makes its point quite effectively even though it uses the "800 pound gorilla" cliché.

Although people justifiably worry about Social Security, paying for old folks' health care is the real 800 pound gorilla facing the economy.[8]

Summary

Let's leave sleeping dogs lie in the bed they made on still waters that run deep. Then we'll pick up some traction like angels dancing on the head of a pin and once and for all recognize that if you want the flowers, you have to shoot for the stars.

Section Three
Selling with Metaphors

"If you were to boil your book down to a few words, what would be its message?"

Chapter 11

Threads: Run a Theme

PETER, A SALES REP for a men's sports magazine (we'll call it *Men's Sports*) had tried for years to win the advertising budget from White & Wilson, a company that manufactured power tools for home improvement. But he hadn't succeeded in persuading Ralph, the brand manager, that men interested in sports were likely to be do-it-yourselfers. Ralph believed that Peter's readers spent their free time watching ESPN or attending sporting events rather than fixing up their homes themselves. Still, Peter wanted to try again; he had new research showing that *Men's Sports* readers were in fact heavily involved in home repair, making them a good target for Ralph's advertising.

He went into the meeting armed with another piece of vital information—he knew Ralph loved to bowl. So rather than rely on statistics alone to win the sale, Peter created a whole presentation around a bowling metaphor. It went something like this:

"Ralph, think of your advertising budget as a bowling ball. For the last several years, you have been rolling it down the same alley—the same home repair publications. You want to hit your target audience, of course—these DIY guys who can't wait to add another power tool to their arsenal. But research I brought with me today will show you that the game has changed. The pins you want to strike are now sitting in a different lane. To hit them, you've got to send that budget ball down a new alley—*Men's Sports.* Let me show you what I mean."

His title page was "Bowling 300: Maximizing Sales for White & Wilson." Key supporting page titles in his presentation included other bowling terms. "The 750 Club: Find Your High Rollers with *Men's Sports*" headed the page of his readers' demographic and purchasing statistics. "Change Your Line-Up" headed a page comparing his readership numbers to his competitors'. "Picking Up Spares" announced additional added-value programs *MS* could offer the company beyond its print advertising. "Strike Now!" was the call-to-action clincher.

Result: Ralph allocated ad dollars to *Men's Sports.*

Why did bowling turn into business? Was the bowling analogy corny? Perhaps to you, but not to Peter's client who loved to bowl. Peter's information made sense to Ralph's decision committee: Joe Left Brain liked the new information and Robin Right Brain loved the extended visual bowling metaphor. A running metaphor casts your presentation material in a different context, one that elevates interest and deepens the absorption of your data.

The Richer the Theme, the Greater the Impact

The key is to select a theme that, like bowling, offers many metaphoric possibilities. Bowling has a vocabulary that lends itself to Peter's vision of Ralph hitting his target at *Men's Sports:* its venue (alleys); the way the game is scored (spares, strikes, doubles, turkeys); the nature of play (having the proper grip on the ball, having proper form); the physical field of play (lanes, gutters); the equipment for the game (shoes, balls, pins); and the rules of the game (dead balls, legal delivery, etc.). Suddenly something as abstract as reaching a readership becomes as concrete, visual, and as loud, as hurling a 16 pound sphere into ten bowling pins.

If, for example, you select a hammer for your running metaphor, you might run into problems. Hammers have a few metaphoric possibilities: hammers bang nails, either driving them or bending them; you can have poor aim and hit your thumb; you can claw out old bent nails to salvage a piece of wood. Beyond that, however, there aren't any visuals to draw on. (Tools would be a better running metaphor, because you could draw on so many to make different points.)

On the other hand, if you select trains as your running metaphor, then, like bowling, you once again have a deep quarry from which to mine your images. Train systems have track lines and trunk lines, express and local trains, express and local station stops, track switches, bridges, and tunnels. There are different kinds of trains: freight and passenger, locomotives and cabooses, flat cars, box cars, sleeping cars, dining cars. Trains break down; they also sometimes derail. Fares are required: there are tickets, ticket counters and booths, and round-trip and one-way fares. And there's more staff: conductors, ticket masters, engineers, men who maintain the track and others who service the train. It's an entire universe, really, with centuries of history behind it to make its imagery accessible to everyone. Which probably explains why the world of trains yields so many metaphors in everyday speech (although the world of cars is right up there)!

Bring Drama to Dry Information

Carol Terakawa, Executive Director of Sales at Yahoo! in Santa Monica, had to present an industry update and forecast in her region to senior management. She was one of several managers making that type of presentation that day. She wanted to do something that would stand out. Since her group covered the entertainment industry on the West Coast, she decided to present her information with a movie theme. Her title page was The "XXX" Strategy—an attention-getting allusion to the movie of the same name. "Lethal Weapon" described one aspect of that strategy. "The Right Stuff" headed a page that described her team. Her "Mystic Pizza" pie chart explained revenue sources. "Field of Dreams: If We Build It, They Will Come" previewed the future. Needless to say, what could have been a very dry topic entertained management and stood out from the presentations of her colleagues.

Summary

- A running metaphor that threads its way throughout your presentation can be a very effective technique for presenting your recommendations and information.
- The best running metaphor threads rely on themes or worlds rich in image-laden vocabulary.

YOUR TURN

From the worlds listed below, select two you feel comfortable mining for material to make metaphors. Write down all aspects that you can think of for each world chosen.

Example: **The World of Cooking**

- What a cook does (selects ingredients, prepares them for use, mixes them, seasons them, sautés or steams, bakes or roasts, grills or fries)
- What a cook uses (pots, pans, knives, graters, spatulas)
- What a cook decides (the pairing of foods, the pairing of wine and food)
- How food is presented (paper plates or bone china, garnishes, family style or nouveau cuisine)
- Kinds of courses (appetizer, palate cleanser, entrée, side dishes, dessert)
- Types of cooks (fast food, short-order, sous chef, pastry chef)
- Culinary disasters (burnt food, fallen soufflés, undercooked meat, over-steamed vegetables, sauces that never thicken, sauces that curdle)
- Food occasions (picnics, Thanksgiving feasts, brunches, birthdays)
- Celebrity chefs (Julia Child, James Beard, Alice Waters, Emeril)

1. The world of gardening
2. The world of war
3. The world of baseball (or your favorite sport)
4. The world of romance
5. The world of cars

Chapter 12

Grabbers: Get Attention

ONE OF MY MOST challenging assignments was a presentations skills program for a group of top new business executives at a national investment management conference. These people spent every day of their working lives making presentations. They earned healthy six-figure salaries. They had sizeable egos and they did not suffer fools gladly. How was I going to get them to pay attention and participate?

"Good morning, everyone," (a safe beginning). "Welcome to our 'Winning Presentations' Program. Let me ask you a question. How many squares do you see on this page? (See figure below)

"Sixteen!" volunteered one person. "Seventeen," said another. "Keep looking," I said. "Oh, twenty-one!" came another voice. Now, everyone was riveted on this figure.

"Very good," I said, picking up a red magic marker to circle them. "But there are more. Can you see the others?" After a few seconds, I said, "Okay, let's see just how many there really are. We all see sixteen.

Where are the others?" Answers flew at me: "The big one!" "The four sets of four in the corners!" "The one in the middle!"

A sea of 'I-dare-you-to-show-me-any-more' eyes flashed at me.

"Right, but there are more: there are also four sets of middle fours and four sets of three by three's which makes the total at least thirty squares," I offered, and wrote a big '30' on the page. "You came close," I added, to protect their clearly bruised egos. "Most people see only up to twenty-one squares."

"Now," I continued, "You're thinking, 'But what does this have to do with our program?' When you looked at this figure the first time, you saw sixteen squares, maybe a few more. No one saw all thirty. Similarly, what you know about making effective presentations is your 'sixteen squares.' Our goal today is to get you to see the possibilities of what you may be missing. You're going to see all the ways a presentation can increase your selling power and bring you more business."

The power of this opening is that it knocked the group off their pedestal of believing they knew all they needed to know about making pitches. The perception game disarmed them enough to pry open their minds to the possibility that there might be more yet to learn about presentations. I was able to link the game to my message. I had no trouble drawing them into the rest of the program after engaging them with this visual sixteen-box metaphor.

How Did I Conceive My Opener?

First, I ran through the Four-Step Metaphor Workout:

1. What was the group's conceptual blindspot?

   They thought they knew it all when it came to presentation skills.

2. What could my snapshot tell me?

   Successful, sophisticated, smart men and women from all over the U.S, experienced at selling investment management services. A driven, highly competitive group short on time and long on ego.

3. What metaphor would most effectively pierce their resistance?

   A sophisticated audience assumes they already know what you're going to say. I would have to challenge them; I would have to show them, immediately, that maybe they didn't know everything when it came to presentation skills. I decided to build an opening that would capitalize on their competitive instincts and challenge their assumptions. The sixteen-square illusion would engage them intellectually without triggering the "heard this all before" shut-down response.

4. How would I relate my sixteen-square metaphor to the subject at hand—making better presentations?

   The link was to stress that they might be missing the potential for more—more boxes, more sales—by assuming they already saw everything. Their current skill level was their "sixteen squares": many more boxes/skills, techniques and strategies might be at their disposal if only they were to pay closer attention to the possibilities.

Why Did It Work?

The Best Opener Is Surprise

My metaphor was a visual surprise—an optical illusion. But metaphors of any sort surprise your audience because by definition, a metaphor is something other than what is expected. It's a stand-in for the obvious. That's why a story about something or somebody works: For a moment, or several minutes even, your audience is treated to a distraction.

I heard a speaker open a marketing conference once with a story he'd heard about a guy on an airplane. This passenger sat next to a woman with a very unusual ring on the middle finger of her left hand. When he commented on it, she said it was her wedding ring. The man asked, "Why do you have it on the wrong finger?" Replied the woman, 'I married the wrong guy.'"

After the laughter died down, the speaker linked the story to his point. "Given the disappointing results we have all been experiencing in the market lately, it is fair to ask, 'Are we married to the wrong guy—the wrong strategy?" He then went on to describe alternative marketing strategies.

A joke surprises by offering a punch line you don't expect; similarly, a good metaphor makes an attention-grabbing opener because it takes the audience where they didn't expect to go. Stories that get everyone to laugh do double duty, because the audience is both surprised and amused. But make sure you can relate the story back to your topic: An unrelated joke may work for Jay Leno, but as icebreakers for presentations, they usually backfire, making your audience more, not less, uncomfortable.

You can tell a story of your own or you can invite your listeners to use their imagination ("Imagine you are waiting for a train...") and the effect is similar: They're momentarily transported away from their assumptions. Likewise, a novel image, an unbelievable statistic, or a little-known fact can snap your audience out of their complacency. Even a question they're not likely to be able to answer right off the bat can do the trick.

Openers Should Never Offend

Always take into account your audience when choosing a metaphor. Surprise them, but make sure your tone and content remain appropriate. In my program, I was addressing high-rollers in a conference room; had it been a boardroom full of stockholders, the perception-game opener would have been inappropriate: too boisterous and competitive.

Be sensitive to generational, cultural and value differences. Frank Sinatra references may go over the heads of Eminem fans. Analogies about the Chicago Bulls may fall flat or arouse animosity if used in Los Angeles or New York. Disparaging comparisons to cell phone abuse may be unappreciated in a company where it is the norm to take cell phone calls during meetings.

A Good Opener Is Just Long Enough to Make the Point

Some openings may be quite short—a question, a startling image, a funny reference. Stories or metaphors that build an image can take longer. But for the opening to work, the metaphor must not ramble; it must offer only enough detail to set up your linking statement.

Imagine you are promoting investment in public education to a group of executives whose children attend private school. They're not likely to identify with the problem of underfunded public schools. Competition, however, is something this group can relate to.

Here's how one speaker opened her plea, standing in front of a huge "14" projected on the wall behind her:

"Good morning, everyone. Let me ask you a question. How would you feel if the US were number fourteen in the world in Olympic hockey?" She pointed to the wall. "How would you feel if your favorite baseball team was number fourteen in its league? How would you feel if you were number fourteen on a standby list to get on a flight? Not too happy, I suspect."

"Yet fourteen is where the US ranks in the world in math among thirteen-year-olds. That is behind Slovenia, Korea, Hungary and France. If we want to stay competitive in the global market, we clearly cannot have our workforce finishing fourteenth in math. We can remedy this situation, but we're going to need your help."

Is there an ideal length for an opening metaphor? The answer to that is the same as the one my tenth-grade English teacher gave my classmate when he inquired how long his book report should be. Mrs. Harris, bless her, replied (metaphorically), "A book report is like a woman's skirt. It should be long enough to cover the subject, but short enough to keep it interesting."

The K.I.S.S. Principle Applies

My sixteen-square figure was quite simple to grasp, if not to solve. More importantly, the **link** I made between the 16 obvious boxes and the group's presentation skills did not require considerable explanation. My audience did not have to work too hard to "see" my point.

Metaphors can make even highly technical material easy for the layman to grasp, provided you keep the metaphor itself simple. Imagine that your topic was the Automated Payment Transaction tax (the brainchild of Edgar L. Feige, a retired economist from the University of Wisconsin). Look at how this opening metaphor pulled people into a potentially deadly topic.

> *Think of your economic life as a highway. It's decently paved. But thanks to the tax system, there are tollbooths all over, with rates so high you need someone along to help you find ways to pay them or plain get around them.*
>
> *Now imagine that a sort of tax-system E-ZPASS comes along, enabling you to whiz through the booths without digging in your pockets or consulting a guide. Suddenly, the highways are opened up and you're no longer wasting time or energy.*
>
> *The Automated Tax System is the E-ZPASS solution to our complicated tax system...*[1]

One image is all your listener can work with at a time, usually. Scott McNealy, CEO of Sun Microsystems, tried to explain current market conditions with a metaphor but clearly got carried away:

> *In the old days, we had an economic cycle that was a nice rolling, gradual curve. Now it seems we don't have rolling waves; we have real edges. The real issue is, can you turn on a dime as the needle starts flipping back and forth?*[2]

(Ummm, we are rolling, we have edges, we are turning on money in response to flipping needles – we are hopelessly twisted!)

In contrast, listen to how this person opened a discussion of the economic downtown of the new century:

> *In Arizona there's an old graveyard known as Boot Hill where lots of slow-on-the-draw gunslingers are buried. One of the battered headstones reads, 'I knew this was going to happen, but not so soon.'*
>
> *The same could be said about the U.S. economy, which has gone through a wrenching contraction. I don't know anyone who thought the hyperbole of 2000 could last, but no one thought things would drop as fast as they did. (3)*

The Ultimate Opener

Imagine you are on the advertising agency selection committee for British Rail in the UK. You have come to Allen, Brady and Marsh, a popular UK ad agency working in the '80s and one of several agencies who might be chosen to handle your campaign. You enter into a dirty waiting room and are virtually ignored by the gum chewing secretary sitting at the desk. You are then kept waiting for 45 minutes. Just as you've decided to leave, outraged at the treatment you've received, in walks the agency executive, who greets you with, "See how upset you are? Ladies and gentlemen, you have just experienced your own product!" The agency then demonstrated the campaign and strategy they would use to win back the hearts, and business money, of BR's dissatisfied customers. Allen, Brady and Marsh won the account.[4]

Summary

- Metaphors make great openers, because metaphors surprise.
- Opening metaphors must be appropriate in tone and content for the audience and the setting.
- Effective openers include only enough detail to set up your point.
- A metaphoric opening clarifies complex topics provided it is limited to ONE image.
- You must link your metaphoric opener to your message.

YOUR TURN

Think of an upcoming presentation or one you recently found rather challenging to put together.

1. Write out the **topic** in two sentences: ______________________
____
____

2. What is (or was) your client's **blindspot**, his expected resistance to your topic? ______________________________
____
____

3. **Snapshot** your client/audience. What information do you have about them? ______________________________________
____
____

4. **Create** a metaphoric opening, keeping in mind what you know about the audience and the setting of your presentation, and drawing on:
   - Articles or stories you've read recently
   - Some factoid or info-bit you found interesting/funny/strange
   - A television program or news headline
   - Something on the Internet that got your attention
   - A common life experience—something frustrating (like computers), something funny (a Lucille Ball rerun), something heartwarming or affecting (Special Olympics)
   - A story, a hypothetical situation, a visual game, or a question to surprise and engage your audience

   Be sure, however, that you link your opening metaphor to your message.

Chapter 13

Anchors: Position Yourself

GREAT! YOU'VE HOOKED YOUR audience: They know why you're there and why they should listen.

Now you are at the point—before you launch into the core of your presentation—where you must position yourself in their minds: who you are, what you do, and how you differ from your competition.

So don't *tell* people. *Show* them.

Brian, a money manager in a seminar I conducted, thought he knew exactly how to describe his firm's value. "We tailor a strategy to your needs," he told me. "We provide excellent customer service. We work to provide consistent long-term returns over time."

Playing devil's advocate, I pointed out that every money manager says pretty much the same thing.

"Yes," he replied, "but we're really good at this."

"So are the others," I countered.

"But we're *better,*" he said, defiance now creeping into the tone of his voice.

"Come on," I pushed. "*How* are you better?"

"We're... we're...like architects!" he blurted out, throwing up his hands.

"Really?" I pressed, intrigued. "How are you like architects?"

"We not only design your retirement, but we manage it as well, so that your financial house" —Brian smiled, pleased with his developing analogy—"always comes together the way you want it to!"

While he was looking very smug I continued, "If you're like architects, what does that make your competitors?"

He thought for a moment and said, "They are like carpenters or electricians. They may be very good at one aspect of the construction job—say, financial planning—but not as good at overseeing the entire responsibility—which includes managing, monitoring, and servicing the client's assets."

Get Angry!

The moment our discourse rises above the ground line of familiar facts, and is inflamed with passion or exalted by thought, it clothes itself in images.

—Ralph Waldo Emerson

Having trouble hitting upon just the right metaphor? The problem is that you're probably not "in your right brain." We live in such a left-brain environment—everything is digital, logical, and linear these days—that it's easy to get locked into a Joe Friday mindset. Yet when we get emotional, more right brain, the metaphors come easily. "Boy, we are in such trouble. *We're toast!*" "The movie was so slow moving. *It was like watching paint dry!*" "Look at that crazy driver. *He drives like a maniac!*" Push yourself and the metaphor(s) will come.

Brian had found his positioning metaphor. He had made his money management firm—a field filled with literally hundreds of competitors—into something people could remember because they could see it. The building of a house, with all its attendant designers and workmen, is something everyone can envision, and that's the key to a positioning metaphor. To make your audience understand and remember who you are, you must give them a visual, whether by invoking a strong image or by teasing out a scenario. The more abstract your job title, the more technical or foreign your business, the more imperative it is that you anchor your description in visual language.

I am the general. My soldiers are the keys, and I have to command them.

—Vladimir Horowitz, Pianist

For instance, FINCA (Foundation for International Community Assistance) is in the business of "micro-financing." But since for most people that is unfamiliar, Deb Burand, Executive Director of FINCA, cuts through the confusion with this image: "Think Citibank for the poor." With these few words she gets her listener to see 1) a large, full-service bank 2) a group of people typically underserved by large banks and 3) how there would be room for another kind of lending organization to step in and help these underserved people get small businesses off the ground. Indeed, that is exactly's what FINCA is and does.

John Mackey, CEO of Whole Foods, the wildly successful natural food supermarket chain, describes his expectations for his premium-priced stores by comparing them to Starbucks. He told *Fortune* magazine he wanted natural foods "to become as common as four-dollar lattes."[1]

Sometimes what you do is so familiar to your audience that you must dramatize it in order to make it meaningful or colorful enough for your audience to retain. When Lisa Yarnell, Founder of Inline Strategies, LLC, is asked what she does, she replies, "I fix sick consumer companies by implementing strategies that move them to healthy profitability." She's in fact a management consultant, but by making us visualize her clients as ailing patients whom she nurses back to financial health, she gives much more unique emotional color to her service.

As a top saleswoman for Steinway & Sons, Erica Feidner tries to ensure that clients investing tens of thousands of dollars in a piano come away with exactly the right instrument. She positions herself instantly by telling potential customers that she is "a Piano Matchmaker."[2]

In addition to anchoring a service in a listener's mind, a good analogy or metaphor can quickly anchor products, people, and even a stock. For instance, a Jeep Grand Cherokee, according to its manufacturer, is a very safe car. But what if you were to think of it—as a recent ad campaign suggested—"as a 4,000-pound Guardian Angel"? As for people, Prime Minister Margaret Thatcher was known variously as The Iron Lady, Attila the Hun, and Plunder Woman. Russell Simmons has been called the Godfather of Hip-Hop. Imagine I told you about a stock that is in an up-and-coming industry, with unlimited potential, very high growth rates, and with proprietary technology. Interested? What if I added, "Think Microsoft in 1984." Now, how interested are you?

Metaphors help others "get" what someone or something is by replacing paragraphs of explanation with a few words chosen for their visual and emotional impact.

The Harry Miller Company invented a shoe that literally grows as a child's foot grows. It stretches two and a half sizes. It needed a name that communicated the concept of expansion, but that was at the same time childlike, or appealing to children. Solution? Borrowing from Mother Nature, the company named the shoe the Inchworm.

Your Distinguishing Metaphor

There are many metaphors that can anchor your product, service or personal uniqueness in the minds of your clients, but they fall into just a few categories.

One Vivid Image

Cisco Systems 3700 router promotes integrated security for corporate computer systems. How does it anchor this product that shields other software and data from hackers? In big red letters, its ad reads "I am a snarling pack of Dobermans.'" (Right! A pack of attack dogs is just what you would want to sniff out burglars and vandals and protect your company's productivity.)

I float like a butterfly and sting like a bee.

—Muhammad Ali

Personification

An abstract concept takes on life—literally—when you can make it into something that lives and breathes. For example, a portfolio manager who was rewarded for making the right stock picks in the tech sector said he was a shepherd—albeit a hard-hearted one—and his stocks were his sheep. "I keep my flock moving along," he said. "If one strays behind, I turn around and shoot it."[3]

The car industry is forever personifying their products. Even the names cars have—Jaguar, or Viper, for example—suggest anything but two tons of inert metal. Here's what Luca Cordero Di Montezemolo, CEO of Ferrari, said of his product:

"A Ferrari is like a beautiful girl that makes you fall in love at first sight."[4]

Turn Descriptive Processes into Familiar Products

Cars, in fact, are so familiar to your audience that they are frequently metaphors for processes or services. Here's how a client of mine described web-page design: "Web design is a tricky business. You can get a beautiful looking result, but if it doesn't work, it's useless, like a Porsche with a faulty engine. We deliver websites that both look good *and* perform well."

You may have to link metaphors to get your process into familiar territory. A courier service describing itself as a firm combining "the speed of DSL with the service of Nordstrom's" anchors itself very clearly and positively in a listener's mind.

There is a new breed of dog called a Labradoodle. Its personality could be accurately described as that of a cross between a Labrador and a poodle. Or, more vividly, it's a dog that "looks and acts like what you'd expect if you plugged an oversized mop into an electric socket."[5]

Use a Story

Stories can come from shared experience, or shared literature, fairytales, the Bible, or mythology. "You remember the story of Icarus?" a software salesperson asks his clients. "He flew too close to the sun and was killed when his wings, made of wax, melted. Well, your staff is relying on software to fly in one very hot marketplace. Our information software won't melt in the heat of competition."

Think in Terms of Miller* Analogies

Graduate students, college students, even high school students are familiar with test analogy questions like:

> *Boats are to water as cars are to_________ usually written as:*
> *Boats:water::cars:*
> *a) gas b) engines c) highways d) steering wheels*

(Correct answer is highways. Boats ride on water and cars ride on highways.)

Analogies rely on parallel relationships. Here are a few examples to help you get the hang of it:

---

*No relation to this author.

- *We are to the car what the car was to the horse and buggy—a revolution in our industry.*
- *We are to our industry what Nike is to sports, McDonald's is to fast food, and what Wal-Mart is to retailing—: Number One in its field.*
- *We are to the specialty chemicals business what Tiger Woods is to golf—the defining player by whom all others are measured.*

Summary

- Before your listener can pay attention, he must understand who you are and what you do.
- Position yourself with a metaphor: It **anchors** who you are and what you do by comparing you to experiences or people already known to your listener.

YOUR TURN

1. What **single vivid image** defines your company?

   We are the/a ______________________ of/in the industry.

2. What **combination of qualities** from known entities would you use to describe your company?

   We combine the ______________ of ______________ with the ______________ of ______________

3. **Animate** a service or product you provide by comparing it to a person or animal.

   Our product/service is like (a) ______________________

4. What parallel relationships can you use to describe your company's position in its industry?

   My company is to the ______________ industry what ______________ is to the ______________

5. Describe a key executive (or team of specialists) in your company metaphorically.

   He/She/They are like..., or a combination of... ______________

   ____

Chapter 14

Nutshells: Make Memorable Recommendations

"To win the war against terrorism, we have to think like a street gang, swarm like a soccer team, and communicate like Wal-Mart."[1]

"Business is like a swim at the beach. If you go with the tide, you go somewhere. If you go against the tide, you splash around and go nowhere. You need to find the tide and go with it."[2]

"States and local governments spent like sailors on shore leave in boom times. Washington should not bail them out now.."[3]

IS THERE ANY DOUBT as to what each of the speakers above is recommending? Their metaphors encapsulate quickly, succinctly, and vividly what is to be done and why.

The thought process behind a recommendation that's rephrased framed with a a metaphor is fairly simple. First, ask yourself: *What am I actually recommending?* Second, determine the problem your recommendation will solve. Third, run through various possible metaphors, selecting the one that communicates most clearly and succinctly what you're urging.

On the next page are samples of metaphors created for common types of recommendations.

Recommendation	Problem to Be Solved	Sample Metaphor
Replace System A with B	Old system is too slow.	In effect, we will be replacing a horse and buggy with a Porsche.
Move from Process A to Process B	Process A needs to be streamlined so that it works more efficiently	Bottom-line, the new process will take the sand out of the gears
Change from Vendor A to Vendor B	Vendor A is not netting the company the kind of prospects it needs.	Vendor B will be like a magnet that pulls out the needles we want from the general-population haystack.
Reorganize to improve collaboration on projects	Communication, morale, and productivity are down.	It will move us from a company of stray shooters to a team of marksmen.

Summary

Recommendations resonate more deeply when they incorporate a metaphor.

YOUR TURN

1. What recommendation to a client have you made recently?

____

____

2. What problem does it resolve?

____

____

3. What metaphor can make that recommendation more vivid in your listener's mind?

____

____

Chapter 15

Burners: Explain, Simplify, Reinforce Points

WHEN SALLIE KRAWCHECK ACCEPTED the job of CEO at Smith Barney, following a series of conflict-of-interest problems at that company, many doubted she could restore customer credibility. Krawcheck assured shareholders she was up to the task. "The public," she explained, "is like a jilted lover. It's going to take some time to win them back." (1)

Her metaphor worked on many levels. Without using the term "betrayed," Krawcheck nonetheless articulated how Smith Barney clients felt in the wake of recent revelations. Instant forgiveness, as with an ex-lover, was not likely. Additionally, however, her jilted-lover metaphor shows that she is acknowledging the company's responsibility as jilter, the one who ruined the relationship—surely the first step toward reconciliation. Finally, the utter frankness of her comparison leads us to believe that whatever subterfuge and evasion preceded her arrival as CEO is history. Krawcheck fully embraces the challenge of rebuilding trust.

In short, with her incisive analogy, this CEO deftly avoided a potentially labored explanation—one which might have cast further doubt on her abilities—and instantly quelled investor anxiety.

For it is with words as with sunbeams – the more they are condensed, the deeper they burn.

—Robert Southey, Poet

More Words, More Confusion

In any pitch or presentation, no matter what you're selling or advocating, explanations are inevitable. Perhaps you must explain how you differ from the competition; perhaps not everyone is familiar with the service or product you provide. Or perhaps you've got a breakthrough process or technology that's quite complex. Conversely, maybe the action you're suggesting to your audience is so obvious and straightforward you need to explain why they haven't thought of it before. Sometimes, you need to explain a fine difference between two apparently similar things. Or—and this is where Sally Krawcheck found herself—you need to explain how you're going to fix something that's broken, that perhaps you broke.

So you explain. You go into great detail. You offer up everything you know, you use the right terminology, you explain the terminology, you leave no stone unturned. It takes time, but you're in earnest.

And yet, it seems, the more you talk, the less people listen. Or they listen but they don't understand. Or they understand so completely they tune out. The more they drift, the more earnestly you explain…and the further they drift.

Explanations needn't involve a lot of words. Explanations that simply train-car adjectives or string together descriptions ("it's back-loaded collateralized emerging-market structured debt") compound the listener's confusion or boredom. Explanations that go on and on about how a screw-up occurred don't minimize the mistake; they draw attention to it. The less said, the better—provided each word you choose triggers in your listener's mind a host of relevant and revelatory associations.

He who speaks well fights well.

—Proverb

That's where metaphor and analogy come in: With an apt comparison, you can **familiarize** the unknown, **simplify** the complex, **reveal** new twists in the straightforward, and **refine** hard-to-see differences. You can **dig** yourself out of a hole; you can **mold** perception before it sets against you. The well-chosen metaphor **focuses** understanding instead of allowing it to diffuse. The perfect analogy **crystallizes** meaning in a visual, intuitive, emotionally poignant way that pierces through resistance to lodge permanently in your listener's brain.

"It's Like Nothing You've Ever Seen…"

Steelcase, the office furniture company, rolled out a new business chair in 2003 called the Catchet. It was like no other chair on the market. The back legs were not forged of one continuous piece of metal: instead, they were jointed in the middle, as if they had "knees." Indeed, they looked like the rear legs of a horse.

Even though the design was a breakthrough in terms of ergonomic comfort, Steelcase knew it was going to need one powerful explanation to sell the thing. The chair so violated expectations of what a chair should look like that customers were likely to reject it out of hand.

Isn't that the irony with innovation? People want to be on the cutting edge; they want the very latest technology; they pine for the next new thing. Time and again, however, when confronted with the next new thing, they resist it tooth and nail. People simply cannot imagine needing or using anything they haven't yet experienced—*unless* it's explained in terms of what they already know and love.

Hence the trick to selling something brand new—something no one has experienced or seen before—is to get your audience to visualize it in the context of familiar images. Show them how it is like something they use now and can't live without. You will succeed not only in explaining it (winning Joe Left Brain's approval) but also in selling it (getting Robin Right Brain to jump up and down with glee).

Thinking of the chair in the context of other once-foreign-now-familiar technologies (computers, cell phones, PDAs), Steelcase hit upon just the comparison—and sold a lot of office furniture. "You've never seen a chair with knees?" read the ad copy for Catchet. "Not long ago, people hadn't seen a typewriter with a TV screen, either."[2]

Of course a chair, however innovatively designed, is still a chair—a familiar object whose functionality and necessity requires no explanation. But what about those technologies that are both cutting-edge AND complex? That are utterly abstract and outside the experience of all but the most techno-savvy?

The whole concept may need to be recast in a substitute set of images and terms. It may need an old vocabulary, one heavy with visual associations, to explain new functions.

The internet is a perfect example. Previously used by academics and the military, this breakthrough technology quickly became known to the masses as "the information superhighway." And yet, that metaphor, with its wonderful image of a ten-lane freeway, wasn't enough to make it a tool for everybody. Every technical term, every function, had to be renamed in order for it to become user-friendly to the public. To make email familiar, programmer-speak was dropped in favor of language that hearkened back to the Mayberry-RFD familiar: "addresses" (summoning the image of your friendly mailman) "white and yellow pages" (as in a good old-fashioned phone book), and "bookmarks" (akin to that slip of paper in your library book).

Eventually, an entire internet vocabulary evolved based on familiar office vernacular. Instead of a "working interface area" or "live memory staging area," we looked at our Inbox. Instead of mail going into "destruction containers," "SMTP acceptance containers," or "communication reception logs," it went into Files. And "tabular user interface" or "structured user interaction table" became, thankfully, simply our Desktop. Strands of hypertext meant nothing to us, but translated into familiar office functions, like chatting and sending mail, the internet became a household phenomenon in a breathtakingly short time.

Simplify Complexity

When things are technically or scientifically alien to your listeners, the best solution is to look for a parallel to something even your grandmother or twelve-year-old nephew would understand. The tendency, unfortunately, is to infuse your explanation with technical terms in order to do justice to the complexity of your subject. But people don't value (or buy) what they don't comprehend. You need an analogy—a metaphor which works on several levels.

One of IBM's products is an integrated technology that solves a company's billing problems. It's an excellent product, but one graphic its salespeople show to explain how the software works can be daunting to explain. It looks like a computer circuit board, with a dizzying array of connecting lines and boxes on it, supposedly demonstrating all of the billing inputs and various outputs that work together to improve productivity and efficiency. When I asked Lisa, a marketer at IBM how she would explain this graphic very simply to, say her grandmother or to a twelve-year-old, she thought for a moment and then the metaphor popped into her head.

"Doing your billing the way many companies are used to," she explained, "is like baking bread from scratch. Things go wrong:

Your liquids are the wrong temperature, or you knead in too much flour, or you don't knead the dough long enough. You wind up with a lot of bread failures, which wastes both your time and your ingredients.

"In contrast," Lisa continued, "using our integrated billing system is like making bread with a bread machine. A company puts in its ingredients, turns on the machine, and gets perfectly risen, perfectly baked bread—and you will get that perfect bread every time. Similarly, that is how IBM's integrated software can save you time and money: by giving you consistent, excellent results."

Science, like technology and finance, can be difficult for a layman to understand. Dr. Carl Anderson, Brookhaven National Laboratory, New York, recognized that when he used this metaphor to explain the importance of two genes that could protect the body from cancer. DNA-PK and p53 are critical components of the body's repair system. "The human genome is like a great castle. In healthy cells, the castle stands strong but as cancer develops, it quickly crumbles. DNA-PK and p53 are the crucial cornerstones that hold the castle up. When they are intact, we are safe, but when either goes wrong, the castle starts to collapse."[3]

Define a Problem

People in the dot-com world tend to have short attention spans. The ability to explain something succinctly is expected. Online media consultant Doug Weaver recognized that when he nailed the depressed dot-com advertising problem as it existed in early 2003.

So this is what it is right now. Even as the online advertising industry continues to make really smart moves, as we develop capabilities that are reshaping marketing as we know it, we're constantly reminded of our most notable—and visible—shortcoming: the advertising environment. It's a bit like the story of Cyrano de Bergerac: The guy speaks amazing verse, but can't catch a break because of that gargantuan shnozz.[4]

Sharpen a Difference

Understanding the dynamics of taxation and allocations in the U.S. is a daunting prospect for most people. When the government says it has authorized funds for a project, how is that different from appropriating funds to see that project completed? And should we care?

Jack Welch, former CEO of General Electric, hit on just the metaphor to differentiate the two terms in our minds.

> *An authorization is usually a 'limiting' number—the legal maximum level of funding. To use a highway metaphor, it is the guardrail that keeps wildly spending appropriators from driving the federal*

budget over a cliff. Only those reckless enough to grind against the guard rail would want to reach those levels.

The appropriation is usually a number that is closer to the median of the road, the realistic figure to do the job.[5]

His clarification doesn't change our deficit, but it will help us understand what the government's up to when it allocates or authorizes the spending of our money.

Defend an Unorthodox Position

When Google, the hugely successful search-engine firm, announced its plans to go public in 2004, the investing community started frothing at the mouth. But those on Wall Street hungry for quarterly earnings were less than thrilled by certain remarks in the company's public offering statement. In very clear terms, Google stated it was not going to offer quarterly earnings. Inevitably the company would make unprofitable short-term investments; Google expected shareholders simply to accept the inevitable. Google justified their position with this metaphor: *"A management team distracted by a series of short-term targets is as pointless as a dieter stepping on a scale every half-hour."*

Defend Value

Helping a client see value beyond price is a particularly frustrating problem in selling. Rather than simply repeat a litany of features and benefits, a more successful strategy is often the use of a hard-hitting analogy to turn your client around. One sales person I know uses the following when he has a resistant buyer client who also happens to sail.

I am not a sailor, but I bet there are various tools and systems you use on a boat that are critical to its operation. Is that right?* (Yes.) *What would be one of them?* (Well, clearly a compass for starters.) *Would you want that to be the cheapest or the best you could find?* (Obviously the best because if you are off by even one degree, you'll wind up far from where you want to be!) *What makes a good compass?* (One that is more tolerant of magnetic interference, works better in salt air, has a better illumination system and is easy to read at different angles.) *Exactly. Our company is like your best compass, the best in the industry. Our systems are solid, able to respond easily to change in

your needs, and are easy for all employees to use. Isn't that worth the investment? Why risk going" off course" with lesser quality?

Justify Looking at Alternatives

How often do you hear, "We are very happy with our current vendors"? Your prospect is hopelessly stuck on his perception that he doesn't need you. Bypass Joe and appeal to Robin: *Mr. Client, Golfers have fourteen clubs in their bag. Each one does a different job. Our service, like those clubs, may complement and strengthen what you are currently doing and make you more competitive in your market. Can we explore some of these possibilities?*

Apples to Apples

You'll notice that explanations are clearest when they rely on metaphors or analogies that are structurally parallel. If you are explaining a process, for instance, your chosen metaphor must be another process—as Lisa did, our IBM employee, compared processing bills to making bread. If you are explaining a marketing strategy, your metaphor might come from other worlds that also use strategies: the military, sports, politics, or even dating. If the confusion stems from how different components work together, then your metaphor will be based on a relationship, such as that between husbands and wives, or coaches and athletes, or members of an orchestra, or players on a team. If your explanation is about how something works—hardware, software, the human brain—then you need to find an analogy to something else mechanical or with moving parts.

For example, how do you persuade senior executives that corporate training should be revamped based on neuropsychological principles? Evidence had shown that employees get more out of training initiatives if trainers adopt different teaching approaches to accommodate the range of learning styles. Training magazine writer Martin Delahoussaye made the case for different approaches by comparing the mind to a radio:

> *Every radio station has a unique transmitting frequency. To achieve perfect reception you tune the receiver to said frequency. If the receiver drifts, even by a fraction, the signal loses some of its sharpness and clarity. More drift brings the fuzzy sounds of other*

stations into the mix. Eventually, the ability to decode the signal is lost altogether. You can't discern words or music any more, just noise. This is analogous to how we learn.[6]

Explaining What You Want—*Quickly*

Benjamin Carson is an internationally celebrated brain surgeon. In a delicate operation, a hole opened up in the patient's channel that carries blood away from the brain and blood began to spurt all over the place. His assistant started to panic. Dr. Carson said, "Calm down. Put your finger in the dike, just like the Little Dutch Boy." The operation continued and was a success.[7]

A client of mine at a leading hedge fund was having a tough time explaining to the low-to-no-tech members of his firm just exactly what Information Technology did for them—how the various IT systems they had put into place were improving communication in the firm. Seeing the confusion on his audience's faces as he fell into the occupational hazard of over-explaining, he cut to the chase by saying, "Basically, we are the arteries and veins of the organization. We ensure that communication of all kinds flows easily and quickly throughout the organization, from the heart of this operation out to its extremities and back again." His audience may not have grasped the technical subtleties of IT systems, but they certainly left with an understanding of how IT improved their efficiency and performance, which was my VP's objective in the first place.

Explain the Counter-Intuitive

A money manager was confronted by an (understandably) irate investor whose portfolio had dropped considerably after run-ups of respectable increases in the preceding years. The money manager reminded the investor that markets fluctuate over time, but historically have moved higher over the long term. The investor was having none of that and continued to complain. Said the portfolio manager:

Think of the direction of the market as a hill. Think of yourself walking up that hill. While you are walking, your portfolio's performance is a yo-yo in your hand. At any given moment, the yo-yo is going up or down, but the general direction of your path is still up the hill. Right now, performance is down, but we believe the upward direction of the market over time gives you the higher performance you seek.[8]

Drive It Home

What you are proposing may not require an analogous explanation; what you're explaining may not be difficult to understand once you've laid out your data. But the more obvious your argument, the more imperative it becomes to imbed it deep in the consciousness of your listener with a pointed comparison.

When asked what happens when Herb Kelleher departs from very successful Southwest Airlines, Analyst Michael Roach from Unisys B2A reassured investors with his response,

***I never thought of Southwest as just the Herb Kelleher show. I look at it like Christianity or Islam. It was started by one guy, but it sure keeps going.*[9]**

Alan Weiss, founder of Summit Consulting Group, is in the business of providing management consulting services to senior executives in *Fortune* 500 companies. When it comes to cutting costs during an economic downturn, he argues persuasively against reducing training budgets, one of the first items usually slashed in tough times, with this metaphor: "No sports team, after a mediocre season says, 'Let's cut back on our coaching staff, our training, and our exercise facilities to save money—that should help us for next year.'" Hard to argue that!

Gary Hamel, strategic management guru, explains why big company mergers do not work. "Whatever the rationale for corporate coupling, a spate of academic research has demonstrated that megamergers are as like to destroy shareholder wealth as to create it. In most cases, the costs of integration, both direct and indirect, overwhelm the anticipated economies…" Then he drives his point home with this clincher: "Put simply, you don't get a gazelle by breeding dinosaurs." (10) (Makes you wish he'd counseled Time Warner before it merged with AOL.)

Minimize an Attack

Fending off barbs by an annoying competitor who is spreading what you believe are untruths about your performance, what would you say to neutralize the attacks? If you were the White House feeling some heat from Michael Moore's anti-Bush movie "Fahrenheit 9/11" and wanted to minimize its importance as well as avoid getting dragged into a discussion about it, you attempted to minimize both Moore and the film by saying, "The eagle doesn't talk to a fly."[11]

Soften the Blow

Some explanations must not only provide an answer but also change an attitude. Krawcheck had to defuse anger and calm shareholder jitters with her answer about rebuilding her firm's reputation. CEOs and political leaders are forever having to wrap their messages in diplomacy, as they're the ones hired or elected to fix the really thorny problems. The best communicators among them know that metaphor is 1) the best way to mold public opinion before it has hardened against them and 2) the easiest way to disarm an audience ready to attack.

Former President Bill Clinton is an acknowledged master communicator. After his talk at the 2004 World Business Forum in NYC on Global Affairs, a member of the audience of 4,000 asked, "In light of current events (the Iraq war), how can the US regain favor in the eyes of the world?" Though not a political event, the forum was probably better attended by Republicans than Democrats. Clinton thought for a moment and then answered, "Like my Mama always said, 'If you want to *have* a friend, you have to *be* a friend.'" That set the tone; just the word Mama disarmed the Bush/Iraq policy-backers in the audience. Clinton then went on to outline specific strategies the US could take to regain its stature worldwide. And, as I looked around Radio City Music Hall where the event was held, even the Republicans were listening because he'd forced them to drop their guard first.

Summary

- When it comes to explanations, quality of expression beats quantity of words.
- Comparisons to the known and loved make the unknown familiar and desirable.
- Simple analogy can make the highly technical easy to grasp.
- The obvious can be made memorable; subtle distinctions can be made more clear.
- Metaphor can frame an explanation.
- Metaphors can change the listener's attitude from negative to positive.
- Metaphors can save explanations from sounding like excuses. The more urgent the need for diplomacy, the more critical it is to package your explanations in metaphor or analogy.

YOUR TURN

Draw three columns.

1. In **Column 1**, list the things you typically explain, e.g., what your product does, how it works, how your firm or product differs from the competition, how you help your clients reach their goals.
2. In **Column 2**, identify the nature of your explanation. Are you explaining a process or methodology? Are you explaining a relationship among parts of a whole, among people, things or organizations?
3. Finally, in **Column 3**, create metaphors that will be most parallel to that thing or process or relationship.

What I Explain	Nature of Explanation	Metaphor

Chapter 16

Shockers: Make Numbers Stick

WHICH HAS MORE IMPACT?

A. *No technology has ever become so ubiquitous so fast as e-mail. It took e-mail a little more than a year to reach its first ten million customers.*

B. *No technology has ever become so ubiquitous so fast as email. It took email a little more than a year to reach its first ten million customers. Compare that to the telephone: 40 years to reach its first 10 million customers; 20 years to reach that mass for fax machines; 5 years for the personal computers."*

Numbers are the ultimate abstraction. Joe Left Brain hears them, but unless Robin Right Brain has a visual context for those numbers, he will have no reaction. For numbers to stick they must be compared to something we can see or touch or imagine, something we know. One year and 10 million customers have no impact—until they're put in the context of other, more familiar technologies' growth.

Eric, an investment banker, was pitching a financing deal to John, CEO of a small shopping center chain. "You know, John, with this financing, we can save you 40 basis points." From the look on John's face, Eric could tell that the savings number hadn't meant much to him. Thinking quickly, Eric added, "That savings is the equivalent of what it would take to build a shopping center for you in the Caribbean." ***Seeing*** **what 40 basis points meant really got John's attention.**

Numbers without comparative context tend to rush through your client's brain like trains that pass through a station without stopping.

How often have you used variations of the statements below in client conversations—and found yourself getting absolutely no reaction?

- "We will save you… (X basis points, Y dollars, or Z weeks of time)."
- "Let me point out to you our increase in…(sales, production, retention rates)."
- "We have succeeded in reducing…(error rates, turnover, downtime)."
- "We have an impressive amount…(of offices, warehouses, dedicated staff)."
- "It will take only (x unit of time) to accomplish our objective."
- "We reach…(two million buyers, six million moms, two hundred thousand doctors)."
- "Best of all, it will only cost…($420,000; $4,200; $420)."

From Abstract to Concrete

To dramatize your numbers so that your audience not only understands them but remembers them long after you've spoken, translate the number into something real. Translation requires you put the number into a different visual context. For instance, say you want to dramatize 300,000, the number of annual fatalities from smoking. What images in your own mental album show mass fatalities? Well, you have visuals for war. You have seen the footage on train wrecks, plane crashes, and sinking ships. You've probably seen movies of towering infernos, mud slides, and earthquakes. Drawing from any of those images, it is an easy step to a vivid equation for your smoking fatalities: "Three hundred thousand people dying from smoking is close to the equivalent of two jumbo jets crashing every day for a year." Yikes!

Verbally Draw the Equivalent

When President Reagan spoke of the trillion-dollar debt, he put it in terms everyone—both economists and taxpayers—could grasp in an instant. He compared it to a stack of thousand dollar bills 67 miles high. (And our deficit today is *how* much?)

An outdoor sign on Broadway caught passer-by's attention with this factoid: "One second of the sun's energy could light up Broadway for 1 billion years." (Talk about the Great White Way!)

Saint-Gobain manufactures 300 square miles of roofing shingles each year—enough, they claim, to build a roof to cover 160,000 American football fields. They make more than 30 billion bottles per year for the food, wine and perfume industries. Laid end to end, that's enough bottles to stretch to the moon fifteen times. (Quite a busy little company.)

Double Numbers' Impact with Celebrated Equivalencies

The wedding industry is a $40 billion industry (that includes dresses, catering, flowers, honeymoon, gifts)—a total that is more than the revenues of McDonald's or PepsiCo and greater than the gross domestic product of some honeymoon destinations (GDP for the Bahamas is only $5 billion).[1] (Ring those [money] bells!)

In 1997, a Lamborghini cost $249,000. That equaled 2 Aston Martin DB7's, 6 SAAB SE Turbo convertibles, 15 Toyota Camry CEs or 29 Hyundai Accents. (How many do you want?)

Stephen King asked for a $17-million advance for *Bag of Bones.* To put that into perspective, Ernest Hemingway received only $16,000 for *A Farewell to Arms.* (Pick up your pen.)[2]

Emotionally Charged Issues Magnify the Result

Is a performance ratio of 99.9 percent good enough? One-tenth of a percent doesn't sound like much until you translate it into outcomes that will make your audience wince. A one-tenth error-rate in, say, health care services means that 20,000 drug prescriptions will be written incorrectly this year, 500 surgeries will be botched this week, and 12 babies will be given to the wrong parents. (Oops.)[3]

American aid to sub-Saharan Africa amounts to less than one-hundredth of one percent of national income—the equivalent of somebody who makes $130,000 a year flipping a quarter to a homeless person once a week.[4]

The world loses approximately one acre of rainforest every second. That sounds pretty alarming already, but consider the impact if you put it this way (as Al Gore did):

> *If, as in a science fiction movie, we had a giant invader from space, clomping across the rain forests of the world with football field size feet—going boom, boom, boom every second—would we react? That's essentially what's going on right now.*[5]

Serial Equivalencies

It's difficult to remember the calorie content of different foods, but not when you read Dr. Howard Shapiro's *Picture Perfect Weight Loss* diet book. Before you grab your next bagel (5 oz. 400 calories) and cream cheese (2½ oz. 250 calories) for a total of 650 calories, consider that you are eating the caloric equivalent of the following combined: four light pancakes, four vegetarian link sausages, two tablespoons light syrup and a dish of sliced star fruit and persimmon. (Good-bye Sunday morning bagels!)

There are about six billion people on the planet. Getting your arms around the qualitative and quantitative differences within that number in terms of ethnicities, relative wealth, health and education is just about impossible. Donella Meadows at the Sustainability Institute in Vermont solved that problem by turning the population of the earth into a community of 100 people.[6] With this perspective, population trends go something like this:

- 61 Asians
- 12 Europeans
- 14 Americans (North and South)
- 13 Africans
- 1 Australian (Oceania)
- 50 women
- 50 men
- 6 people own 59% of the entire wealth of the community
- 13 are hungry or malnourished
- 14 can't read
- 7 are educated at the secondary level
- 25 struggle to live on US$1 per day
- 47 struggle to live on US$2.00 per day

Think about that the next time you think you are having a bad day.

Summary

- Numbers are abstractions that register dramatically when they are put into a visual context.
- Comparisons that are metaphoric—visual, emotional, palpable—make numbers into concrete, memorable impressions.
- To make your numbers shock, surprise, and stick:
  - □ Use vivid images
  - □ Translate them into well-known entities
  - □ Draw on emotionally-charged issues for comparisons

YOUR TURN

What key numbers (percentages, quartiles, dollars, market share, completion times, costs, awards, other) do you typically include in your sales conversations and presentations...

To establish credibility? ______________________

____

To sell benefits? ______________________

____

To explain some process, problem, or outcome? ______________________

____

1. Select those numbers that are particularly important to your arguments.
2. Now make them concrete and boost their shock value with a comparison.

ABSTRACT NUMBER______________________
Vivid image ______________________
Comparison to well-known entity ______________________
Link to emotional issue ______________________
Colorful serial equivalency ______________________

ABSTRACT NUMBER______________________
Vivid image ______________________
Comparison to well-known entity ______________________
Link to emotional issue ______________________
Colorful serial equivalency ______________________

ABSTRACT NUMBER______________________
Vivid image ______________________
Comparison to well-known entity ______________________
Link to emotional issue ______________________
Colorful serial equivalency ______________________

Chapter 17

Seducers: Titles That Tease

IMAGINE YOU ARE A materials buyer at General Motors. You see sales presentations every day—every business out there wants to nail a contract with a firm as large and esteemed as GM. As you settle into your seat for yet another PowerPoint slideshow by another hopeful vendor, a title flashes on the conference room screen that actually makes you eager to see what follows. Is it:

- *"Proposal for General Motors by Innovative Plastics"*
- *"Increasing GM's Market Share"*
- *"Revving Up Sales at GM"*

"Proposal for General Motors" is of course accurate, but it doesn't engage. Its promise to the listener is, *this is going to be a by-the-book presentation* (i.e., terminally boring).

"Increasing Sales for GM" is stronger. It promises a bottom-line benefit, and that's something to perk up the ears of any manager.

The third title, however—"Revving Up Sales at GM"—adds visual power simply by using a verb that speaks to us metaphorically. "Revving" sparks a chain reaction of associations: We see a souped-up car, we hear the throaty roar of its powerful engine, we perhaps experience a surge of adrenalin. Suddenly sales figures take on a sound, an energy, an excitement. We can feel and hear them revving up. *Buckle up, listeners!* says this title. *You're in for an exciting ride!*

Tap Industry Associations

"Today a new name has to work overtime to slice through the clutter," observes Steve Rifkin, marketing strategist and author of "The Making of a Name." "A new name has to hit the trifecta—it has to be distinct, memorable and meaningful. A lazy name is the kiss of death for a marketer."

That sentiment applies equally to your presentation titles. Your title must slice through inattention. Once again, the Four-Step Workout you practiced in the previous section can help. You already know what you're up against in terms of a blindspot: It's safe to assume of your audience that their main objection to your pitch is that they don't want to sit through it. Either they're short on time, or they believe they've heard it all before. Now for the snapshot: *What do you know about your audience?* They all work for the same company, so they're all versed in the language of their industry. Consider what you know about their industry. Write down all the associations you can make.

For instance, say you're presenting to the marketing executives at Marriott Hotels. You want to sell them on the benefits of a database marketing service. There's not a lot of imagery in those words—database sounds duller than binary code, and marketing is what everybody is selling. However, you do know that Marriott is in the hospitality business. What can you do with that?

Think about how hotels measure success. In the hotel business, industry jargon includes terms like vacancy rates, rack rates and "heads in beds." The last phrase is a natural metaphor to use in an opening title:

More Heads in Beds
Increasing Sales at Marriott
With JRB Database Marketing

With a little more imagination, you could extend the hotel metaphor to your subtitle. Think about what the hospitality business is about: home away from home, a cozy bed for the night. What do you picture? A king-size bed? Fluffy pillows? Crisp sheets? Getting a good night's rest? Now think about what you're trying to sell to this group of executives. You have a way to boost their occupancy rates. It's a database you're selling, but it translates into more heads in Marriott's beds. So instead of your first slide saying, "Sales Proposal for Marriott," or even "Increasing Sales for Marriott," stick with your image and its vocabulary:

More Heads in Beds
Plumping Up Sales at Marriott Hotels
With JRB Database Marketing

Your title must, of course, be engaging but also descriptive of what you're recommending. A client of mine, the team at Accessor Capital Management, makes a presentation that helps underscore for their client the difference even a one percent change in a contribution rate can make in terms of return on investment over time. The difference can be as dramatic as having $700,000 to retire on at age 85—or *$2 million.* They illustrate that difference with a very simple but powerful title, one whose image hits the listener at gut level:

Caviar or Catfood?

If they wanted to extend the metaphor, the title could easily be:

Caviar or Catfood?
How Today's Contribution Sets Tomorrow's Table

In either case, the metaphor in the title pulls us in immediately.

Take a Lesson from Book Publishers

Effective presentation titles are like best-selling book titles: They both grab and inform your audience with just a few image-laden words, energetic verbs, or emotionally charged references. Publishers of business books certainly grasp the importance of metaphor when it comes to titling yet another treatise on management practices. As *The New York Times* pointed out in "Recipe for a Best Seller: Analogies about Cheese or Anthills or Parenting," many of the most successful book titles rely on very un-businesslike comparisons—to sports, war, Shakespeare, Antarctic exploration, even peanut butter and jelly. To name but a few:

- *Leading at the Edge: Leadership Lessons from the Extraordinary Saga of Shackleton's Antarctica Expedition*
- *Who Says Elephants Can't Dance? Inside IBM's Historic Turnaround*
- *Who Moved My Cheese? An Amazing Way to Deal with Change in Your Work and in Your Life*
- *Pigs at the Trough: How Corporate Greed and Political Corruption are Undermining America*

In each instance what empowers the title is an image, one freighted with appropriate connotations. If a picture is worth a thousand words, then the image of an elephant twirling on its toe says it all about IBM's turnaround. The image of pigs instantly communicates greed and dirt. With images this strong, the subtitle doesn't have to explain very much.

Bottom line: Take a page from the publishing industry sales manual. Turn to metaphor to make your titles communicate worlds.

Let the News Inspire You

Notice as well the headlines in newspapers and magazines. They tend to be heavily metaphoric because, like yourself, they must grab the attention of an audience pressed for time and communicate the essence of the story in a few words.

- *IBM: From Big Blue Dinosaur to E-Business Animal (2)*
- *The Euro: High Wire Without a Net (3)*
- *Will Godzilla Defeat King Kong? (Verizon's Cingular Threat) (4)*

Summary

- The opportunity to engage your audience begins with your title. It's your promise of what is to come.
- Metaphoric titles engage and inform your audience because metaphoric language is packed with associations—whole images and experiences your audience can draw on in an instant.

YOUR TURN

Review the titles of a recent PowerPoint presentation or hand-out. Does it whisper "another predictable boring lecture" or does it shout "AND NOW FOR SOMETHING COMPLETELY DIFFERENT!"? Try energizing the title with words or verbs that conjure appropriate images or experiences for your client.

Current Title ______________________________

A. Client's/Audience's Industry/world ______________________________

____

____

B. What is the benefit of your overall recommendation or message to your audience? ______________________________

____

____

C. What images do you associate with your client's industry or world? ______________________________

____

____

D. How might that imagery be used to illustrate the benefit of your recommendation or message? ______________________________

____

____

E. Create a dynamic presentation "title that teases:" ______________________________

____

____

Chapter 18

Sledgehammers: Headlines That Hit Home

OUR GENERAL MOTORS' BUYER, intrigued by "Revving Up Sales at GM," sits back in his chair expecting to be engaged. Don't disappoint him. Don't turn his enthusiasm for what you have to share into regret that he ever let you in the room.

In short, don't torture him with a series of "Horse Charts."

What is a Horse Chart, you ask? So did I, when I first heard the term from one of my seminar participants at GTE. "It's very simple," he explained. "You show a picture of a horse and then, over it, you insert a headline that says, 'Horse.'"

Presenters do this all the time. They have great data worked up into charts or graphs or diagrams, and then they label the data with something so obvious you wonder if they gave the presentation to their eight-year-old to finish.

Let's get back to your GM buyer. If you have a graph showing a drop in consumer spending, which headline turns your graph into a Horse Chart?

1. "Consumer Spending"
2. "Consumer Spending Drops"
3. "Buyers Hit Brakes on Spending"

Number 1 is the guilty culprit here. It describes the graph without adding any meaning to it. Now contrast the lifeless "Consumer Spending" to the other two headlines. The second at least communicates your point: the graph illustrates a downturn. But the third headline, which relies on metaphor, has much more impact because it's visual and adds mental color to the actual facts on the chart.

Presentations frequently use charts or tables to make comparisons. I see these charts labeled, stunningly enough, "A Comparison of Option A and Option B." Do this to your General Motors buyer and he will pass into a torpor. You can do better! He will pay some attention if you label the comparison, "Option A Superior to Option B." But he'll listen up even more if you headline the chart, "Option A Trumps Option B."

Take a look at how advertisers label their visuals. They rarely describe just what you're seeing. For instance, BMW wants to sell you its Z4, and a photograph of the car figures large in its ads. But below the picture of the car are the words, "Land Shark." (A horse-chart headline would have been "The All-New Z4.") People likely to be interested in the Z4 know it's loaded, because it's a BMW. They expect outstanding specs—the 6-speed manual transmission, the premium sound system, the one-touch top with heated rear windows. But it's the image-laden Land Shark description that closes the sale emotionally by implying this car will give you the power, aggression, and respect associated with a shark.

Summary

- Headlines should amplify, not explain, whatever information you're presenting visually (charts, diagrams, a series of bullet points, etc.).
- The literal visual information plus the headline's figurative language satisfy both Joe and Robin.

YOUR TURN

1. Review the slides or pages in the body of a recent presentation where you've given a visual some kind of label. Select five key pages.
2. For each of these five pages, can you come up with headlines that expand on the data rather than simply describe it? Can you use metaphoric language to reinforce your point in each instance?

Current headline ____________________

Metaphoric headline ____________________

Current headline ____________________

Metaphoric headline ____________________

Current headline ____________________

Metaphoric headline ____________________

Current headline ____________________

Metaphoric headline ____________________

Current headline ____________________

Metaphoric headline ____________________

Chapter 19

To Communicate Concepts

IF YOU ARE MAKING a pitch that involves clothing, cruise vacations, or construction, you will doubtless insert photographs into your PowerPoint presentation: models wearing your clothing line, vacationers enjoying their cruise, bridges or buildings you have built. With such pictures your viewer can quite literally see the benefits of these products or services.

But what do you do if you have to sell the value of something as intangible as outsourced administration of Employee Benefits? What do you do if you are ADP, which provides outsourced integrated HR/Benefits/Payroll administration services? Do you flash slides of bullet points? Blocks of text? Graphs? Charts?

You could. But you run the risk of boring your audience to tears. There's nothing worse than watching a presentation you have to read. (Actually, there is: listening to the presenter read the bullet points out loud while you read them silently to yourself, twice as fast.)

A better choice is to present an actual picture—a cartoon, an illustration, a photograph, a diagram or schematic—that illustrates *metaphorically* the value of what you cannot literally show.

ADP's advertising campaign solves the problem by showing what I will call a "metaphoric visual"—a picture or illustration that's not the actual thing you're selling (because there is no way you can picture the actual service or product) but a stand-in, or substitute, for your intangible. The ADP ad features a photograph of an executive, exasperation showing on his face, trying to fashion a paper clip from a piece of wire. "Make Your Own Paper Clips?" reads the headline. Below, the text completes the analogy. "No? So why would you do HR Administration in-house?" The ad goes on to explain the benefits of working with an outside provider of these services. And the point is made: Just as making one's own paper clips is a complete waste of an executive's time, so too is administering human resource benefits programs in-house.

When you think Michelin tires, you think safety. Why? Not because of its heavy text descriptions in its ads, but because of one well-known image: a baby sitting on a tire. That one image communicates the *concept* or *feeling* of safety and security they want you to have. Seeing the image, you get their message immediately—even without reading the explanatory text.

A picture really is worth a thousand words, particularly when it comes to communicating invisible concepts like safety, ease, strength, efficiency, danger, and flexibility. And frankly, even when you can be literal with your images, you should consider figurative alternatives. It's an emotion you're trying to kindle first, along with the logic of your argument, and a metaphoric visual will get Robin to vote in your favor.

Consider how unrelated, at first blush, is the image the alternative energy company Exelon uses to promote alternatives to fossil fuels: a picture of a wire basket loaded with eggs. Exelon is in the business of developing nuclear, solar, and wind-powered utilities. What do eggs have to do with utilities? Nothing. But the picture is a metaphor, one which Robin "reads" correctly as, *Don't put all your eggs in one basket*—and relying on fossil fuels exclusively is doing just that. "If ever there was a time to get all our energy from one source," reads the headline under the basket of eggs, "this isn't it."

The more invisible the concept you're selling, the more important it is that your presentation relies on metaphoric visuals. How do you sell, for instance, "a balanced approach to risk management?"

Not only is risk management a tough concept to communicate; you've also got to show how your firm does it better than any other. American Electric Power sells this concept of what they bring to risk management with the picture of an acrobat from the famous Cirque du Soleil troupe. Dressed in an eye-catching costume, the performer balances on one hand atop a pole, her other limbs extended out for balance. Robin Right Brain, without having to resort to words, understands in less than a second that the risk of her falling is offset by her innate balance and extensive practice. "It's all in the approach," reads the headline. (In smaller print, should Joe want factual explanation, is a discussion of how AEP relies on the right internal checks and balances to help a company manage its risk.)

Remember, that as a presenter your metaphoric visuals may not require text at all. You are talking, after all, while your audience is looking at your slide show. This means that whatever needs to be said or explained can be done so by you—no need to burden your slides with words that force your audience to read while they look and listen.

In one of his seminars, Alan Krinsky, search and client relationship consultant to ad agencies and corporations, describes today's increasingly complicated relationship between agencies and their clients, particularly in their views regarding fees and value. He uses a single cartoon depicting crossroads with arrows going in different directions. There are no words on the slide. Instead, he provides the commentary in his remarks. That way, his audience's right brain can appreciate the concept in the cartoon while their left brain gets to devote its full attention to his verbal explanation.

Summary

- When you are pressed to present concepts that are utterly invisible, come up with visuals that communicate that concept metaphorically.
- Resist the temptation to spell out what the metaphoric visual means. Your headline can reflect this metaphor, or you can leave words off the slide and simply talk to your audience about what they're viewing.

YOUR TURN

1. What pictures, images, or cartoons would you use to represent each of the following ideas or concepts?

2. Try for three each for each concept.

   Example: **Productivity**
   1. A chicken sitting on a mountain of eggs
   2. A yard full of rabbits
   3. A stopwatch

   Increased profitability:
   1. ______
   2. ______
   3. ______

   Speed:
   1. ______
   2. ______
   3. ______

   Threats:
   1. ______
   2. ______
   3. ______

3. List the concepts on the left that you hope to communicate in your next presentation. Then brainstorm pictures, illustrations, or cartoons you could use to capture those concepts. List them in the right-hand column.

Your Concepts	**Picture/Image/Cartoon**
______	______
______	______
______	______

Chapter 20

Props: Add Impact

IN 1960, AT THE height of tensions with Soviet Russia, Premier Nikita Kruschev expounded to the world in a United Nations speech his country's position with regard to global supremacy. There was no mistaking the threat in his tone. And then he reached down, picked up a shoe, and pounded the lectern with it. "WE WILL BURY YOU!" he shouted above the din.

Even those who today have no idea what he said remember his message. The image of a premier rapping his heel on that lectern before millions has become one of the major symbols of the Cold War.

More recently, in his run for Governor of California, Arnold Schwarzenegger—the very portrait of might—waved a broom to symbolize his intention to sweep Sacramento clean of cronyism. And In Costa Mesa he had a wrecking ball fall from a six-story crane to smash into a Buick. This was to illustrate his intention to destroy the tripling of Gray Davis's auto taxes. Long after the election his constituency remembers these images (which may not be a good thing if he reneges on his promises!).

Politicians have at their disposal some pretty impressive symbols (George Bush arranged for the battleship *Lincoln* to be his landing site after American troops toppled the statue of Saddam Hussein in Iraq). But bigger is not necessarily better when it comes to props. The smallest props can engage your listeners by involving them in a vivid, visceral way. They see what you mean because they are experiencing it.

When to use a prop? There is really no *wrong* time. As you'll see in the following examples, a prop can lever you into a client's busy schedule, secure his attention, underscore your points, act as a clincher to your presentation, or remain with the client as a constant reminder of your product or pitch.

To Get Appointments

One sales rep I know sends a single Nike sneaker to a hard-to-see prospect with the note, "Want to get our foot in the door. Matching sneaker is yours when we meet." Another sends a small rubber skeleton with a note that begins, "I'm dying to meet you" and ends the note with a promise that he'll be calling to set up an appointment.

To Set the Stage for a Presentation

When Yahoo! held a dinner with security analysts the night before its annual meeting in 2003, it gave each of the attendees a set of juggling balls. The balls were to reinforce the point that Yahoo! had stabilized its finances and was now "juggling" several opportunities for growth. In the prior year, the internet company had distributed yo-yos to make the point that what goes down must also come up.[1]

Paper Bags Lead to Big Bucks

How do you get the attention of charitable givers when most of us receive ten, twenty requests for money in the mail every week? City Harvest—the New York City based organization that collects unused food from restaurants and corporations and re-distributes it to more than eight hundred food programs in the city—does it with a paper bag. They literally send you a folded-up paper bag. When you unfold it, the copy says in bold text, *Most likely having enough food to fill this lunch bag isn't a big problem for you. Not everyone is so lucky.* Then, in smaller text it explains its mission and requests a donation. It is mighty difficult to ignore this dramatic request for donations.

As you can tell, I am a big fan of *New Yorker* cartoons, which I've used to set the theme for each section of this book. A cartoon in a presentation can be a very powerful metaphoric starter. It not only gets a chuckle from Robin and lowers your listener's defenses, but it sets the theme for your message. For example, change is a constant in business. If you are introducing any type of change in your organization, in your deliverables to clients, or if you are making a competitive pitch, show the cartoon below along with the opening following it:

"Sir, the following paradigm shifts occurred while you were out."

Opening Comment:

This cartoon captures what is happening everywhere in the world. Nowhere is this shift truer than in our industry with the advent of increased competition, more demanding clients, and new technologies. Traditional methods no longer work.

How are we going to meet this challenge?

We propose the following:...

To Advocate a Cause

When GOP leaders threatened to eliminate the Public Broadcasting System (PBS), Congresswoman Nita Lowey (currently member of the powerful House Appropriations Committee) "invited" Muppets Bert and Ernie to the congressional hearing to help sell the case for public television. The worldwide publicity that followed, thanks to Bert 'n' Ernie, was largely credited with saving PBS.

To Pound Home Your Points

When a seminar participant in Sydney had to explain why it was wiser to commit to a six-time advertising contract rather than do a one-time test and wait to see the results, she used a hammer, nail and block of wood to make her point. She asked her client to hit the nail once with the hammer and then to try to pull the nail out, which he did easily. Then she asked him to hammer that same nail six times into the wood. When he couldn't pull the nail out, she said, "Exactly. This is like your advertising. When you advertise once, you do not imbed yourself into the consciousness of a reader. You may as well save your money. But when you advertise six times, you get so deep into the mind of the reader there's no way for him to get your ad out of his head. You stand a much better chance of making a sale." So did she: Her prospect signed on the spot for six ad placements.

To Replace Routine Financial Presentations

A purchasing agent unhappy with this manufacturing company's haphazard buying practices and eager to bring about purchasing practice change quickly did the following: On the Boardroom table, he piled samples of 424 different gloves which were used at the company with their different prices. When executives were called in, they could "see" instantly the obvious potential for waste and savings. This visual demonstration created the urgency for change that a list of charts and figures had thus far failed to do.[2]

In Closing

When one online direct marketing salesperson extolled the virtues of e-mail over direct mail for increasing business, he compared it to the speed of a hare vs. the speed of a tortoise—and distributed small toy rabbits to everyone at the end of the presentation as a tangible reminder of his point.

Not a Props Person?

If you like the points the props make, but cannot see yourself actually using the props, then simply create the same metaphors verbally.

1. ***Advertising once and expecting to make an impression on readers is as futile as hammering a nail into a block of wood only once. The nail does not go very deep and is easily pulled out. Similarly, your message will not penetrate and will be quickly lost. However, like hammering that nail six times into the wood, your six time advertising campaign will definitely make a deep impression on your target market.***
2. ***Imagine a child who cannot fill even a paper bag with enough food for lunch every day. Now multiply that by a million. Pretty sad situation, isn't it? City Harvest fills those bags daily, but we cannot do this without your help.***

Summary

- A prop can be a very dramatic reinforcement of your point.
- Props, like good metaphors, need to:
  - ☐ Make your point
  - ☐ Be relevant to the client
  - ☐ Be appropriate in tone and content

YOUR TURN

1. How could you use one of the following to open your presentation?
   - ☐ Golf club
   - ☐ Tennis racket
   - ☐ Baseball mitt
   - ☐ Basketball
2. How could you use one of the following to illustrate a difference between you and your competitor?
   - ☐ Box of cookies
   - ☐ Deck of cards
   - ☐ Dice
3. How could you use one of the following to conclude a presentation?
   - ☐ Wristwatch
   - ☐ Paint brush
   - ☐ Lucky charm (e.g. a rabbit's foot)

Chapter 21

Clinchers: For Dramatic Take-Action Closings

AS A LISTENER, WHEN a presenter says, "In summary…" what do you expect to hear next? A re-cap of key presentation points? Certainly. A call to action? Usually. But do you expect to hear about marriage, sports rankings, or 16 squares?

Circle Back to Your Opening Image

An effective closing is one that loops back to your opening. The "I married the wrong guy" story that hooked our earlier speaker's audience at the outset could easily be reprised in the summary.

> *In summary, from a marketing point of view, we do not want to find ourselves 'married to the wrong guy.' I encourage you to do everything possible to ensure that your corporate marketing strategy is aligned with your customers' expectations.*

The "wrong guy" image would reinforce his key message and add urgency to the call to action.

Remember our presenter who opened with the number 14 behind her on a PowerPoint slide? Her closing remarks might have sounded like this:

> *In summary, fourteenth place is unacceptable in sports, fourteenth place is unacceptable in productivity and, as you've seen, fourteenth place is unacceptable in education for the U.S. Your contribution to local schools both in money and in volunteerism can move us to where we belong: First place.*

When I use my sixteen squares example to open a program, I make sure I revisit it at my closing as well.

In summary, when you return to work and face client demands for new and better solutions to their problems, use the presentation techniques and strategies you learned here. Step back. See beyond sixteen squares and you will find the answers you need to grow your business.

Conclude with a New Metaphor

It's not wrong to introduce a new metaphor into your closing. Your opener may be too distant, too thin, to invoke again; you may need the power of a fresh image or story.

For example, I *could* close a presentation on the power of metaphor by summing up my points: "In summary, you want to be an effective communicator. You've seen that becoming a master of metaphor will strengthen your ability to get your ideas across. I encourage you to use these verbal tools beginning on your very next sales call, business meeting, or public presentation." But consider the impact quotient of this:

In closing, let me share with you the story of the man who prayed to God every day to win the lottery. Every day he failed to win. Finally, after three months of earnest prayer, he became exasperated with God and complained, 'I have been praying to you every day to win the lottery! And yet, I still haven't won. What do I have to do to win?!' Suddenly, the clouds parted and a loud voice boomed down. 'For heaven's sake,' it said. 'Buy a ticket!'

You, too, must "buy a ticket." You cannot expect to win someone's business if you're not playing the game constantly with metaphors.

Here's another, shorter close:

You cannot steal second base without taking your foot off first, right? Similarly, you're not going to gain any ground with a client if you cling to what you've been doing, just hoping this time will be different. Lift your foot. Flex your metaphor muscle. Run for that next base. Start making comparisons immediately—on your next sales call, at your next meeting, or in your next large group event—

and before you know it, you'll be scoring business home runs far more frequently.

Summary

- Ideally your closing metaphor circles back to the image or story you invoked at the beginning of your presentation.
- Any closing is more memorable if clothed in imagery. Use metaphor to underscore your message and stir up the emotion necessary for your client to take action.

YOUR TURN

1. What is the opening you've chosen for an upcoming presentation?
2. What key points will you be summarizing at the close?

   A.____

   ____

   B.____

   ____

   C.____

   ____

3. Use the imagery of your opener to recast these points:

   ____

   ____

   ____

4. Now try recasting them using a whole new metaphor:

   ____

   ____

   ____

Section Four
Metaphor Maintenance

WHETHER YOU PLAY SPORTS, music, or sell, as a professional you constantly work to perfect your performance. Here are three ways to reinforce your metaphor-making powers.

- Observe & Connect
- Travel to Other Worlds
- Become a Clipper

"I was on the cutting edge. I pushed the envelope. I did the heavy lifting. I was the rainmaker. Then I ran out of metaphors."

Chapter 22

Observe and Connect

YOU'VE HEARD THE PHRASE "movers and shakers." Metaphor-makers are "observers and connecters." They are curious beings who notice and register everything around them all the time. They can see similarities in ostensibly dissimilar things. They can connect seemingly unrelated ideas and concepts to new situations. They are sometimes called lateral or parallel thinkers, as opposed to being strict linear thinkers. All of us have this natural curiosity to one degree or another. The key is to feed and develop it.

Before you can do things differently, you have to think differently.

—Rolf Smith, ex-US Air Force Office of Innovation

The Three-Foot Jellyfish

For example, what can you do—metaphorically—with a three-foot jellyfish called "Big Red" to help make your sale or convey your message?

Such a creature was recently discovered in the Pacific Ocean. I learned that from watching *National Geographic* television as I was huffing and puffing on the treadmill at the gym. This creature existed over 250 million years ago, before dinosaurs, and apparently it doesn't fit into any known species. Scientists were amazed to discover this prehistoric inhabitant in today's oceans.

Now, a nonobservant nonconnector would have watched the show, wondered at the jellyfish briefly, and then forgotten about it as soon as time was up on the treadmill. However, observers and connecters (like you) would take mental note, recognizing that the unique or unusual is in such short supply that it deserves brain storage space for future use.

Lincoln studied and appropriated to himself all that came within his observation. Everything he saw, read, or heard added to the store of his information...No truth was too small to escape his observation...

—Joshua Speed, Lincoln's closest friend[1]

For example, you could use Big Red...

...in a presentation

You say you have never heard of us. Well, have you ever heard of Big Red? (No.) Big Red is a three-foot-long jellyfish, part of a species estimated to be older than dinosaurs, that's been around for more than 250 million years. Scientists have only just discovered it. ***We're like Big Red.*** *You may have never heard of us, but we're big and have survived the competition, not for millennia but certainly for a long time. We can more than adequately handle your needs.*

...to counter an objection

You say there is no need to see me because you already know all about my company. May I ask, do you know about Big Red? (No) Big Red is a three-foot-long jellyfish that's been around since before the dinosaurs. Scientists only just discovered it, because they thought they knew all there was to know about jellyfish. I've got some ***Big Red*** *discoveries to share with you in my company—some amazing developments that I wouldn't want you to miss. Can we get together so that I can show them to you?*

...to stand out in a crowded field

You ask why we're recommending you switch to a system platform that's been around for years. Well, ***this system is like Big Red.*** *Big Red is a three-foot-long jellyfish that was recently discovered deep in the Pacific Ocean. It's still around after 250 million years because it's bigger, tougher and more adaptable than all other species of jellyfish that have evolved since. Similarly, this system is still around because no one has designed one better.*

Anything in the hands of an observant, connection-seeking communicator becomes grist for the metaphor mill.

How can a food processor describe what technology has done to the industries that make up our economy? Here's how a writer at *Business Week* linked the two:

***Technology is the economic Cuisinart of the '90s, chopping, mashing and mixing once-discrete industries into new configurations for the consumer's edification.*[2]**

Fine-Tune Your Radar

Every day for the next week assign yourself something to look for that, on most days, you wouldn't notice.

- Count how many people are wearing red at your office.
- Walk down your street but instead of looking at the buildings, notice the roofs.
- On your way to work, concentrate on noticing everything very carefully: what you see, what you hear, feel, smell, touch.
- Can you find five round objects on your desk? Five square objects in your office?

Broaden Your Horizons

- Skip the predictable sitcoms on TV and watch a show that takes you into other worlds—nature, biography, history, the arts, psychology, medicine—where you can be challenged, awed, and/or educated.
- Subscribe to an online newsletter or publication outside your field of work. Subscribe to a futurist newsletter.
- Attend a lecture or workshop on a non-job-related topic which is of interest to you. Sign up for an improvisation class, or a talk on architecture. Take up a musical instrument. Local colleges, museums, and adult-education programs offer classes on everything from Ancient Egypt to How to Do Commercial Voice-overs.
- Plan a day-long nature hike
- Watch a car race, a ballet performance, an auction.

George Carlin can be outrageously offensive in his humor, and he is also an outrageous lateral thinker if ever there was one. One of his more benign observations:

There are women named Faith, Hope, Joy and Prudence. Why not Despair, Guilt, Rage, and Grief? It seems only right. 'Tom, I'd like you to meet the girl of my dreams, Tragedy.'[3]

Lighten Up!

A relaxed mind having a good time is a more creative mind, because Robin is free to play. Encourage his inclination:

- Play a board game with a child.
- Watch a John Cleese video, TV show, or movie.
- Rent the movie Aladdin.
- Watch the old Lucille Ball or Sid Caesar television shows.
- Catch a Jerry Seinfeld comedy special, or just tune in to the comedy channel for some out-of-the-box thinking.
- Look for the oddball wackiness in everyday life.

Commit to Metaphor-Muscle Fitness

Which of these can you pledge to do more of?

____ 1. I can be more curious. I can notice more things, people, places, sounds, smells around me.

____ 2. I can read more offbeat publications, books and internet sites.

____ 3. I can develop more interests, e.g., sports, performing arts, science, history, psychology, collecting, other.

____ 4. I can attend one workshop, lecture, or seminar a year in a field outside of my job.

____ 5. I can watch cultural/historical television, e.g, *National Geographic*, The Discovery Channel, PBS, etc.

____ 6. I can cultivate a more inquiring mind, e.g., "Why is X a certain way? What would X be like if it were done differently?"

____ 7. I can be more open to new ideas.

____ 8. I can indulge my sense of humor and playfulness more often.

____ 9. I can allow myself more time to go down many paths to get to a solution.

____10. I can broaden my mix of friends.

Chapter 23

Travel to Other Worlds

You're the top. You're the smile
Of the Mona Lisa.
You're the top.
You're the Tower of Pisa.

—Cole Porter

COLE PORTER'S LYRICS ARE metaphor-making at its best: There are 21 of them in this hit, all of them more colorful ways to say, *"You're the top!"* Porter draws on architecture (the Coliseum), geography (the Nile), famous leaders (Mahatma Gandhi), animation (Mickey Mouse), food (Waldorf salad, turkey dinner), horse-racing (Derby winner), comedy (Durante's nose), horticulture (rose), literature (Shakespearean sonnet, Dante's Inferno), and dance (the nimble tread of Fred Astaire). Can you "top" those?

Cyrano de Bergerac, the famously large-nosed protagonist of Edmond Rostand's play, is about to kill a man who has challenged him when he hears the man refer to his nose as merely "large." So lacking in imagination was this insult that Cyrano is compelled to correct him.

"Ah, no young sir!" he exclaims.
"You are too simple. Why, you might have said—
Oh, a great many things!"

And he proceeds to describe his nose as a "rock, a crag, a cape, a peninsula," as a "perch" for birds to stand and sing on, as a "typhoon when it blows" and "the Red Sea, when it bleeds."

Rostand, like Cole Porter, is a man with more than one metaphor in his holster—a good defensive strategy for anyone eager to persuade. There are times when your first shot isn't as effective as you'd like, and you need backup. It's like taking pictures at a wedding. To ensure you get your shot, you'd better take more than one.

Being able to draw on metaphors from a number of different worlds is a talent not limited to songwriters or poets. You may be a fashion designer, but that doesn't mean you can't draw a metaphor from the world of cars. Masters of metaphor tour a variety of worlds in their minds quickly to hit upon the comparison that best makes their point.

It's interesting to note that sports and cars are among the most surefire sources of imagery in America, perhaps because we're obsessed with performance. Bear in mind the words of one college professor:

"To understand America, you must first understand baseball. Baseball is not only America's favorite pastime, but the most pervasive athletic metaphor in the American language. Right off the bat we bat around a few ideas and then go to bat for someone. If we don't touch base with others, we may find ourselves way off base or not able to get to first base."[1]

Below is a list of worlds whose dynamics and vocabulary are known to most clients you'll encounter. Circle five of these where you have some working knowledge.

Transportation	Theatre	Science	Wall Street
Television	Internet	Romance	Flea markets
Nature	Sports	Opera	War
Parades	Fashion	Health	Economics
Movies	Technology	Shopping	Crime
Weather	Spying	Architecture	Politics
Mining	Hiking	Farming	Machines
Engineering	Flowers	Holidays	History
Agriculture	Circuses	Languages	Fire-fighting
Parenting	Cooking	Games	Astronomy

Family
Antiques
Education
Manufacturing
Scouting
Pregnancy
Art
Crafts
Math
Medicine
Dance
Cars
Literature
Children
Wine
Volunteerism
Languages
Parenting
Travel
Genetics
Music
Forestry
Plumbing
Love
Law
Pet care
Writing
Design
Yoga
Cities

Drawing on each of the worlds you circled, see if you can come up with three metaphors to describe

- Speed
- Danger
- Success

For example, three ways to communicate **Speed:**

A. (from Wall Street) *as fast as electronic funds transfer*
B. (from Music) *as fast as the 'Flight of the Bumblebee'*
C. (from Nature) *like a hummingbird's heartbeat*

Now you try:

- Speed

  ___
  ___
  ___

- Danger

  ___
  ___
  ___

- Success

  ___
  ___
  ___

Chapter 24

Become a Clipper

When a dramatist places a gun on the table in the first act, the astute playgoer knows that the weapon will be used before the drama ends.[1]

WHAT A GREAT OPENING line! The imagery is so potent, so engaging. I immediately cut this out and filed it away for future use. It might help me persuade a client to take action now, rather than later, in response to a seemingly small shift in his industry. I could make the point, with this quote, that companies who survive are those who perceive the gun as a threat long before it's fired.

I've got a quite a box of gems like these. I clip and file them according to what larger point they make, so that when I'm desperate for a grabber of an opener, or a clincher of a closer, or a thunderclap to drive home certain points, I need only consult my folders. I have hard-copy files and computer files, depending on how I come upon my metaphors. Most come from the newspapers and magazines I subscribe to, but whenever I hear a catchy description or apt metaphor I jot it down. I also collect good visuals: cartoons, ads, and illustrations that strike my right-brain fancy in some way. Periodically I visit them to see if they can be adapted for an upcoming presentation or sales situation. Sometimes the clippings just serve as a springboard, helping me to arrive at my own perfect metaphor.

As a master of metaphor, you, too, will become a clipper. You'll find that just keeping your eyes and ears alert for new material will awaken you to a world sparkling with them. The more of them you pick up and pocket, the more trained your eye and metaphor making skills will become. Then two things will happen. 1) You'll be able to take what you find and use it to dazzle an audience into seeing things

your way. And 2) when you reach for a metaphor to save a sale, more often than not you'll find one right at hand—without having to turn to your collection.

Make It Your Own

What would you do with the following?

In a different age and under vastly different circumstances, the late Chinese leader Deng Xiaoping once talked about crossing a raging river by "feeling the stones underfoot." All of us—including George W. Bush, his war council and his economic advisors—are in that river now, trying to feel the stones.[2]

There are lots of possibilities. You could use it to explain what it will feel like as your colleagues try to adjust to a new system, or a new administration—after, say, a merger. Employees don't change or adapt overnight: Finding their footing in the new order is a lot like crossing that raging river. These days, technology is moving so fast that you could apply this image to a lot of firms struggling to reinvent themselves. Kodak, for example, has got to move from making traditional cameras and film products to products that support digital photography. That's a real treacherous crossing. I might use this river image, alternatively, to defend why it is important to really "get under the surface" of a problem. If a client wants to realize success on a project, just feeling the stones underfoot may not be a good-enough strategy.

Here's another of my favorites:

In the 1970s and 1980s one often read about remote mountain villages where people stayed healthy and vigorous into their 90s, with some individuals reaching extraordinary ages. How did people in these simple, traditional societies achieve such longevity? The answer, it turned out, was that people in simple, traditional societies aren't very good at counting.[3]

I love the way this story takes a ninety-degree turn with its image of village peasants. From afar, we imagine their longevity to be the result of some transcendent lifestyle choice. Up close, we find these people to be as flawed and as subject to aging as we are.

So, while the story itself isn't a metaphor, I can see using it metaphorically. I might use it to open a meeting on why people should do their own research, or refuse to take someone else's findings at face value. Maybe I'd tie it to the larger—and fairly disturbing—trend among big companies to be overly reliant on analysts' reports.

Here's one more sparkler from my files:

> *The telecom crisis is reminiscent of a classic scene in "The African Queen." Humphrey Bogart and Katharine Hepburn, desperate and lost on the Ulonga-Bora River, rip pieces of wood off the little steamer and use them to fuel the vessel's engine. Today's telecom companies, struggling to survive one of the greatest busts in business history, are slashing prices below cost and selling precious assets. Neither one is a long-term survival strategy.*[4]

This writer used the imagery from this beloved movie to describe, metaphorically, how the telecommunications industry is cannibalizing itself. What an eye he had for analogy! I saw the same movie and failed to register the scene well enough to mine it for metaphor. But no matter: There's no reason it can't be used again in a different context. I can see using it, for example, to justify why a client should hire an outside firm rather than "rip pieces of wood" from itself by using up its already overworked staff. What comes to your mind?

Read Movie Reviews

Movie reviews are rich in metaphors and are a good metaphor textbook for salespeople. When the apparently dreadful movie *Gods and Generals* opened in March 2003, critics had a metaphoric field day. *The New York Times* collected choice reviews from around the country and Canada:[5]

As dry as a high school history book, solemn as a funeral service, humorless as a Politboro meeting, bloated as a waterlogged corpse, and unbalanced as a bout between a debutante and a sumo wrestler.

—The Charlotte Observer

General Boredom meets Major Tedium on the Civil War fields of Virginia.

—Toronto Globe and Mail

This is waiting-at-the-Bureau-of-Motor-Vehicles-long, the sort of long that has you…checking your watch furtively as 216 golden minutes of your life are slowly, painfully strangled.

—Portland Tribune

(Guess we can safely skip that one!)

I even clip things I like but don't need immediately, such as "a diamond is a chunk of coal that made good under pressure." This is clearly a case of Robin winning out over Joe in my brain.

My Metaphor Vault

When you're stuck—and it happens to all of us—the clipping file can be a godsend. Looking through it, you'll find just the quotation, or story, or image you need, or you'll feed your right brain enough fuel to kick Robin into high gear to come up with a fresh metaphor.

While you're building up your own reserves, feel free to take what you need from my own vault. I've been banking metaphoric material for years. I make no apologies for the eclecticism of the collection, drawing, as I do, from seminar participants, friends, speakers, articles, advertisements, speeches, sayings, magazine articles, and the internet. It's organized according to the larger point I think the clip makes, but again, feel free to use as you see fit. Sources are noted wherever possible.

ACTION/RESULTS

As one goes through life, one learns that if you don't paddle your own canoe, you don't move.

—Katharine Hepburn, actress

Even if you're on the right track, if you just sit there, you're going to get hit.

—Will Rogers, satirist

One stands for long time with open mouth before duck flies in.

—Chinese Proverb

The time to fix the roof is when the sun is shining.

—John F. Kennedy

APPETITE (Positive)

I'll tell you what kind of boss he (Bob Hope) was: insatiable. There were never enough jokes. We didn't call them jokes. We called them 'crumbs for the bear.'

—Mort Lachman, "Bob Hope Before He Became an Establishment," *The New York Times* 4/20/03

APPETITE (Negative)

Being asked to speak before your peers is like being the javelin competitor who won the toss and elects to receive.

ATTITUDE

If you think you can, or, if you think you can't, you're probably right.

—Henry Ford

CHALLENGE
The problem is that you are selling Star Wars technology to people with buggy-whip mentalities.

It's like trying to change the oil in a speeding car.

It's like running a race with a ball and chain around one leg.

The sharks are circling. Will we be diners or bait?

It's like riding a tsunami with a surfboard.

The bubble's burst.

CHANGE (Positive)
We are beginning to get traction..., see the light..., pick up speed...

CHANGE (Negative)
We're not in Kansas anymore, Toto.

—Dorothy, The Wizard of Oz

The party's over...

The good times hit a brick wall...

Like a driver who accidentally slams on the brake instead of the accelerator, the stock market boom has come to a screeching halt.

As passé as tail fins, poodle skirts and saddle shoes

As useless as last week's ticker tape

The cream is beginning to curdle

The honeymoon is over

What drove the rapid expansion in trade and capital flows was the notion that the world was becoming a seamless, frictionless place. Now, there's sand in the gears of cross border connectivity. That's a huge tectonic change in the global landscape.

—Morgan Stanley's global economist, "What's at Stake," *Business Week* 10/22/01

CHAOS
Like a zoo with all the cages left open

Like rush hour in Grand Central Terminal

Like a pinball machine gone berserk

A (fiscal, human, business, scientific, etc.) train wreck

Like a Greek tragedy. Everyone does what he thinks is right and the result is chaos.

COMMITMENT

We are known to stay the course

Like marriage partners, we are in this for the long run

COMMUNICATION

Clinton has "emotional acuity"—a talent for projecting ease and empathy, an ability to size up a person or a group of people, sense the vectors of hope and sentiment or anxiety and resentment rocketing around the room, and windsurf the breezes and gales of feeling toward his goal.

—Hendrik Hertzberg, *The New Yorker*, 10/16/04

Speech must be as bold as a lion, soft as a gentle hare, impressive as a serpent, pointed as an arrow, and evenly balanced like a scepter held in the middle.

—Tibetan Proverb

COMPETITIVE LANDSCAPE

Like a jungle where only the fit survive...

Like a dogfight, where you have to outmaneuver the competition, respond quickly to change, and ultimately prevail...

Like chess, where you have to plan your every move...

What was once a polite tennis match has become a boxing match with multiple opponents, each one working hard to score a knockout.

It's as if we're on the interstate at 5PM on a Friday afternoon.

CONFIDENCE

Nobody can make you feel inferior without your consent.

—Eleanor Roosevelt

CONSCIENCE

I cannot trim my conscience to fit this season's fashions.

—Lillian Hellman

CONFUSION

It's hard to tell whether the dog is wagging its tail or the tail is wagging the dog.

It's like driving in fog without a yellow line to guide you.

It's like waking up in a hotel when you're on a multi-city business trip and not being sure what city you're in.

Explaining hedge-fund indexes is like blind men feeling an elephant. The man in the front thinks he has a hose, another one a tree trunk and the third a wall, while the guy at the end says he is tugging on a rope.

—"Tracking Hedge Funds; An Inexact Science"
The Wall Street Journal 9/17/03

DANGER

X is our exploding cigar

Like unexploded landmines

The canary in the mine is gasping for air

DECIDING

When a client said, "I can't decide," one consultant responded, "You're sitting on the equally attractive horns of a dilemma. It's like asking which is more important, food or water? You need both."

At a crossroads

DIFFERENCE

As different…
as a whale is from a goldfish
as a yacht is from a barge
as dawn is to dusk
as summer is to winter
as the Himalayas are to a hill
as a chain letter is to a love letter
as a candle is to a halogen light
as a cold is to pneumonia
as couture is to off-the-rack
as Rolex is to a Timex

DIFFICULTY

Like growing violets, which are easy to kill because they are so delicate, we must be careful not to…

Negative people are toxic to a staff's morale. It is wise to let them go before an epidemic of negativity breaks out.

Like walking on eggshells

Like an elephant trying to balance on a tightrope

Like eating soup with a fork

As difficult as putting barbed wire into a paper bag

Like trying to nail jello to the wall

Like shaving whipped cream off an inflated balloon

Like trying to catch the wind

Like mounting a defense in a paper fortress

Like going through a revolving door with a surfboard

Like wrestling an octopus

Like pulling a tooth from a wildcat

It's going to be as easy as pushing a camel through the eye of a needle

It's going to be like dragging a safe through the sand

Hercules could not have budged….

DISCIPLINE

In 1999, the difference between the leading money winner on the PGA tour (Tiger Woods) and the guy who came in dead last was less than two strokes per round. But that 1.8 strokes per round translated into several million additional dollars of earnings. Consistent practice and discipline pay off!

DISTINCTIVENESS

If you dressed in black and white and then entered a room full of people dressed in black and white, what would be your chances of standing out? None. But enter in a red dress and everyone would notice. The same holds true for your __________ Just add__________ to your current___________and you'll be amazed at how you stand out from the crowd.

DROP IN PERFORMANCE/SUPPORT

Plunged like an elevator out of control

Dropped like a rock from a ten-story building

Dropped like a stock after bad earnings are announced

EMOTIONS

Eager as prisoners on their first day of freedom

Constrained, like a person in a straitjacket

As sad as a cocker spaniel without its master

ERROR

Like a camel: the result of a decision by committee

FEAR

It's like a snake's rattle. It scares people off.

Frozen like a deer caught in the headlights.

Like the feeling you get in the pit of your stomach on a turbulent flight.

FINALLY TURNING THE CORNER

Out of the woods

Seeing light at the end of the tunnel

FLEXIBILITY

Roll with the punches

Ride the waves

A reed in a windstorm

Have wiggle room

FORECASTING

You can't tell who's naked until the tide goes out.

GROWTH

Multiplying like rabbits

Spreading faster than an internet virus

Like watching time-lapse photography of a tree growing

HARD TIMES COMING
Buckle up. It's going to be a bumpy ride.

Beware of landmines.

Icebergs lie ahead.

Like balancing on a high wire without a net

What was the wind at our backs has become wind in our faces…

…is a time bomb (e.g., An aging population is a demographic time bomb which will destroy our economic growth if we don't plan for it.)

IMPACT
Like a tsunami

IMPOSSIBILITY
Even Sea Biscuit couldn't win a race with a 400 pound jockey on his back

IMPROBABILITY
Like lovemaking between porcupines

INATTENTION
Husbands are like fires. They go out when unattended.

—*Zsa* Zsa Gabor

INCOMPETENCE
It's like dogs chasing cars. They love to chase them, but don't know what to do with them when they catch one.

INEFFECTIVE STRATEGIES
Doing business without advertising is like winking at a girl in the dark. You know what you're doing, but nobody else does.

—Stewart Henderson Britt,
New York Herald Tribune, 10/30/56

As futile as shouting in a storm

As hopeless as telling a teenager to clean up his room

As useless as chicken wire stopping bullets

As useless as last week's ticker tape.

As pointless as a hook without bait

As foolish as expecting a racehorse to win without a good jockey.

As disillusioning as discovering that a great seafood restaurant gets its tuna from a can.

You wouldn't buy a car in parts. You buy it whole. Why would you piece together your software system from different software component manufacturers?

Like elephants mating: lots of noise and clouds of dust and then nothing happens for a year.

Rearview mirrors are good for driving, but not for investing.

INEVITABILITY
You cannot put the genie back in the bottle.

You can't fight City Hall

INSPIRATION
This is America...a brilliant diversity spread like stars, like a thousand points of light in a broad and peaceful sky.

—George Bush, 1988 Republican National Convention

Shoot for the moon. Even if you miss it, you will land among the stars.

—Les Brown, motivational speaker

INTERNET
Huge data pipes make up the backbone of the internet

The information superhighway

The internet is to school research in the '90s what the calculator was to math in the '70s.

—AT&T WorldNet President Dan Schulman,
"Yakkety-Yak" Yahoo! Internet Life, 1/99

IRRELEVANCE

A male gynecologist is like an auto mechanic who never owned a car.

—Carrie Snow

Doing________would be like using a hornet's nest for a piñata: not recommended.

A woman needs a man like a fish needs a bicycle.

—Gloria Steinem

LEADERSHIP

Leaders without people to support them are like musical conductors without an orchestra. No matter how proficient the conductors may be, no music can be made and nothing will happen.

LUCK

Get up early. Work late. And strike oil. —John D. Rockefeller

Luck is preparation meeting opportunity. —Louis Pasteur

MEDIA

Television is chewing gum for the eyes. —Frank Lloyd Wright

NEGOTIATION

You cannot shake hands with a clenched fist. —Indira Gandhi

OPPORTUNITY

If someone gave you the winning lottery ticket, would you take it?

If a $100 bill flew into your hand, would you toss it away?

If someone had a diet that worked, would you ignore it?

This is like the "Antique Road Show." You're sitting there with real value and you don't realize it.

If you want to catch trout, don't fish in a herring barrel.

ORGANIZATION

Like clothes strung out on a line

As efficient as a major league baseball team

Like a bee hive: seemingly chaotic, but highly organized and productive

As hierarchical as the army

As separate as silos

PATIENCE

It's like setting up a retail outlet. You took time to figure out where to locate your latest store. If you didn't do all the appropriate research, your risk of making a very expensive mistake was high. The same is true of what we do. We do our homework. It takes time to do it right, but we spare you some very expensive mistakes.

It's like the pilot doing his preflight checklist. You want him to go through that list as carefully as possible. If he rushed it, he might miss something, and in an airplane that usually means dire consequences. Similarly, we.... to ensure that everything gets off the ground in good order.

Open-heart surgery takes hours. Rush it and you may as well have never started it: You'll do more damage than good.

It's like turning a battleship around 180 degrees. We can do it, but it will take some time.

PERFECT SOLUTIONS

"______" is the Holy Grail of ___. Everyone would kill to get it.

Our mix of ___ is like winning the trifecta/Super Bowl/World Series

It's the Oscar, Emmy, and Tony all rolled into one.

PERSEVERANCE

When life gives you lemons, make lemonade.

If you want the rainbow, you have to put up with the rain.

Before you can have the view, you have to climb the mountain.

How do you get to Carnegie Hall? Practice, practice, practice.

PERSPECTIVE

It's like a stained-glass window. You have to step back to get the full effect.

It's the Rashomon effect. Everyone has a different view of what happened.

POOR QUALITY

Madonna has made a dash of talent go a very long way, like stretching a Chiclet to the moon.

—Letter to the Editor, *Vanity Fair,* 12/92

PRECISION

Like operating with a scalpel, not a meat-cleaver

With the precision of a piano tuner

As precisely as a marksman who takes aim with only one bullet in his rifle

With the care of a person packing her own parachute

PREVENTION

It's a lot cheaper to get your teeth cleaned twice a year than to undergo root canal work—and a lot less painful.

PRICE

If you were having a pacemaker put in, would you want the $2,000 model or the $6,000 model? Clearly the latter. And that is why people pay a premium for our....

Suppose you were moving. Would you pay someone to drive a car or a truck to haul your furniture? While the car might be able to haul one piece at a time and do it cheaply, as a practical matter, that would hardly pay. Our value is that we provide the necessary power to help you get the job done quickly and efficiently. Therein lies our value.

Why are we worth more? It's like the story about the plumber who charged $18 to fix a leak under a sink. He tightened a bolt to do it. "Eighteen dollars to tighten a bolt!" exclaimed the house owner. "That's outrageous. It was only a bolt!" "Yes," said the plumber, "but I knew which bolt to tighten." Similarly, we have the experience to know exactly how to approach....

Our costs are like electricity: You pay only for what you use.

Launching an e-commerce site without a portal partner is like opening a retail store in the desert. Sure, it's cheap, but does anyone stop there?

That approach/strategy/policy is like cotton candy. It's sweet, but when it's gone, all you're left with is a bellyache.

PROCRASTINATION

An international crisis is like sex. As long as you keep talking about it, nothing happens.

—Harold Coffin, *Reader's Digest,* 9/61

PURPOSE

It is not enough to be busy; so are the ants. The question is, what are we busy about?

—Henry David Thoreau

RARITY

Like a polar bear in the jungle

As unimaginable as plastic covers on Martha Stewart's furniture

Like snow in August

READINESS TO ACT

Armed for battle...

Hit the ground running...

RECURRENCE

It's like a boomerang; it keeps coming back.

RELIEF

A weight off your shoulders

Water in the desert

RESPONSIBILITY

The buck stops here.

If you can't take the heat, get out of the kitchen.

RESULTS

Our service will revolutionize the way you ________ the way penicillin transformed medicine: It's going to ensure your survival.

RISK

Like playing with a chemistry set and not reading the directions.

SIMILARITY

As alike as buttons on a shirt

Like grapes in a cluster

Like peas in a pod

SIZE

An ego the size of Texas

As big as…
…12 football fields,
…the Astrodome
…a 747 jet
…a Broadway stage
…Lake Michigan

As tiny as an infant's fingernail

As thin as an eyelash

A mile-wide smile

SPEED

You get your response back in less time than it takes to blink

X passed Y as if X were driving a Porsche and Y a Schwinn

STANDARDS

Good enough never is.

—Debbi Fields, Mrs. Field's, Inc.

STRENGTH/WEAKNESS

A chain is only as strong as its weakest link…

Reagan was often observed to be the Teflon president. Nothing bad ever stuck to him.

Like bullets off a Sherman tank

_____ is their Achilles heel

Women are like teabags. You never know how strong they are until they get into hot water.

—Eleanor Roosevelt

SUCCESS
To eagle the first hole

To hit a home run

To ace the serve

To win the Triple Crown

What Crayola is to crayons

What Nike is to sneakers

What Microsoft is to software

SURPRISE
Like having the ladder kicked out from under you

Like winning the lottery

Surprises are good for Cracker Jack boxes, but not for ____

SURVIVAL
Dodged a bullet

TENACITY
Like a bulldog gnawing on a bone

Enough shovels of earth: a mountain. Enough pails of water: a river.

—Chinese proverb

Push the envelope

Go the limit

Each time a man stands up for an ideal, or acts to improve the lot of others, or strikes out against injustice, he sends forth a tiny ripple of hope. And crossing each other from a million different centers of energy and daring, those ripples build a current which can sweep down the mightiest walls of oppression.

—Robert Kennedy, University of Cape Town, 1966

THINGS NOT WHAT THEY SEEM
Like Richard Cory, the man who seemed to have it all, who went home one day and committed suicide

Like refrigerator magnets: they only look like food

Like a Venus Flytrap: alluringly scented but deadly

Like a mirage in the desert

UNATTRACTIVENESS

All the style of a UPS truck…

As pleasant to the ear as fingernails scratching a blackboard…

As popular as an army of ants at a picnic

As welcome as a plague of locusts/a case of poison ivy/a hungry Grizzly

UNCERTAINTY

The debate is not so much whether the Dow Jones Industrial Average will cross the 8000 mark, but whether the milestone will serve as a new blast-off point, a grazing pasture, or a cliff.

—*The Australian,* 1997

UNDERSTATEMENT

Baseball, it is said, is only a game. True. And the Grand Canyon is only a hole in Arizona.

—George F. Will

UNINTENDED CONSEQUENCES

Fancying herself quite a catch and flirting with George Bernard Shaw, dancer Isadora Duncan said to the great dramatist,

Imagine a child with my body and your brain

To which he replied,

Yes, but what if it had my body and your brains?

UNITY

I believe a house divided against itself cannot stand. I believe the government cannot endure permanently half-slave and half-free.

—Abraham Lincoln

Like a married couple, we have to work hard together to raise this family of firms to maturity.

URGENCY
The economy that was the wind at our back has become a wind in our faces. It is necessary to revisit the way we do business.

It's like a battleship with gaping holes in its side. No matter how big and powerful it once was, it is going to sink now if things aren't fixed quickly.

Even a Mercedes needs a tune-up on a regular basis.

It's like having a few termites in your basement. Put off exterminating until you see a colony, and your house will be sawdust.

Even if you're on the right track, if you just sit there, you will get hit.

—Will Rogers

VALUES
In the end it always comes down to one's values. As Buddha says in verse 121 of the Dhammapada, "Do not think lightly of evil, saying, 'It will not come to me.' By the constant fall of water drops, a pitcher is filled; likewise, the unwise person accumulating evil little by little becomes full of evil."

—Daniel Vasella, CEO, Novartis,
"Temptation Is All Around Us," *Fortune* 11/18/02

WEAKNESS
A house of cards built on a base of quicksand

WINNING
When you win, nothing hurts.

—Joe Namath, Football Legend

Conclusion

WHEN I asked one of the consultants in this book for permission to quote him, he said with a sigh, "I think of myself as such a big thinker *and all that people remember are my analogies and stories!*"

If you were paying attention for the last hundred and sixty pages, that is *precisely* the point of this book.

Metaphors are among the most powerful weapons of mass understanding and retention you have to wield on the plain of competing products, services, and ideas. They belong in all your communications. Whether you are closing a deal, motivating a group to take action, or seeking to bind a nation to your vision, metaphors will smooth your way to the results you want. As this Arabic proverb, with a slight twist, says:

> *He is the best speaker (and salesperson) who can turn men's ears into eyes.*

Appendix

25 Stories from Metaphorians Like You

1. Opposites Attract in Love, Life, & Language
Catnip or Caviar?
Ladder or Jungle Gym?

2. Why Settle for One?
Jack Be Nimble, Jack Be Quick
No Ceiling on Metaphors
Tigger or Eeyore?
Ride That Cyclone!

3. Once Upon a Time
It's a Small, Small World
Bait Your Blog
The Tall Poppy Syndrome
The PIN Code

4. Beginner's Success
Engage Me or Die
JFK, Zorro, or Wonder Woman

5. News You Can Use
Arab Spring
Blood Is Quicker Than Water
President Obama's State of the Union

6. It Doesn't Have to Be Dull, Trite, & Boring
A Cliché a Day Keeps the Buyer Away
Down by the Seashore
What Color Is Your Hat?

7. Take Them Out to the Ball Game
What Inning Are We In?
Batter Up!

8. Spontaneous Eruption
Where Is the Next Party?
What's a Ferrari For?

9. When Idols Fall
Humpty Dumpty Woods

10. When It's Personal
Twist the Kaleidoscope
Picking a Few Bones

1. Opposites Attract in Love, Life, & Language

Catnip or Caviar?

A portfolio manager distinguishes between the return an investor can expect using an asset allocation strategy vs. a straight stock selection strategy by saying, "The choice you make between these two strategies will determine whether you eat caviar or catnip in your retirement years."

Hold the catnip, thank you. Bring on the caviar.

In a world in which whatever you're saying can sound very similar to what the next guy is saying, using opposing images helps you underscore your point. The media is full of such examples.

- Discussing how the fortunes of GMAC soured shortly after a $7.2 billion infusion of capital from private equity firm Cerberus in 2006, Allan Sloan in *Fortune* captured the essence of the disaster by saying, "The ink had barely dried when GMAC's mortgage business, much of it subprime, turned from a crown jewel into toxic waste."
- In a *Time* article on President Reagan, the writer noted that as a boy, Reagan's hero was Franklin Roosevelt. But Reagan's thinking changed radically over the years, and as a politician he led a crusade for conservative government. While Roosevelt established political norms that lasted half a century "...the life jacket of one generation can become the straitjacket of the next...."
- Joe Klein in *Time* observed that Obama completely reversed the American political calculus of the 1980's and '90's. "He made the Democrats the party of optimism and the Republicans the party of root canal."

The Take-Away

Opposing images crisply define options for your audience and help position one of them as obviously superior. Create your own opposing metaphors or adapt these examples to fit your situation:

Do you have to describe the advantages of one process, approach, methodology, or system over another? "*Program A will energize your employees while Program B will make their work feel like a root canal.*"

Do you need to argue for or against different options: "*Which new hire will become our crown jewel and which will become toxic waste?*"

Are you advocating a change from the status quo: "The clients that *once served as our life jacket have become a straitjacket as their businesses have gone overseas.*"

Ladder or Jungle Gym?

WHAT do you say to make yourself sound unique and fascinating when you are asked to introduce yourself at a business or social event? If you are Barbara Marks, graphic designer turned painter, you say, "My life to this point has been less a ladder and more a jungle gym. Many people have linear careers, knowing exactly what direction they want to pursue, but mine has had many more lateral moves, swinging from one branch to another, maybe more like a jungle, to mix metaphors."

Interested in hearing more?

We were. Barbara was a guest at a select senior business dinner, and her metaphor immediately grabbed everyone's attention. She led us through her jungle gym career—starting with her anthropology major at college, then her job as a graphic designer, which turned into her role as entrepreneur. An interest in painting and drawing then took her to classes at the Lyme Academy College of Fine Arts, which she loved so much that she ultimately gave up her business to become a full-time painter. The idea of graduate school popped up later. She thought, "Why not?" and off she went to get her MFA. Now she is exploring the relationship between painting and poetry—and has talked herself into a poetry course at Yale.

The Take-Away

There were eighteen of us at that dinner. When it came their turn, everyone else offered up the plain vanilla version of who they were and how they got there. Barbara's story with her contrasting metaphors is the only one that remains with me.

2. *Why Settle for One?*

Jack Be Nimble, Jack Be Quick

FRANCINE Smilen sells a variety of leadership and professional development programs to buyers in companies that range from fashion to finance. Like most sellers, one of the biggest challenges Francine faces is helping prospects really understand what her firm does.

Says Francine, "It is hard for buyers of training to understand our unique business model. I represent fifteen different companies in the learning industry who provide programs and services—from classic behavior modeling to fully customized programs, and everything in between.

- "If I'm working with prospects in financial services, I describe myself as a 'financial advisor.' My job is to meet with organizations to determine their learning needs over their organizational life cycle and to make the right recommendation to meet those needs from among the programs/services that we offer."

- "If I am in the fashion/retail industry, I describe our work as being 'like a stylist'—depending on the client's needs, we can offer everything from the plain white tee shirt to the couture gown."

- "In health care, I refer to myself as a 'primary care physician' who keeps the big picture in mind and calls in the experts as needed."

"These simple comparisons to jobs my prospects can relate to make it easy for them to grasp what we do, and paves the way to bigger and better business opportunities for me."

The Take-Away

You can be as successful as Francine. Just think: What does my company do? What is it like in my listener's world? Then, forge the connection between the two in your prospect's mind to create instant understanding. The more you train yourself to think like this, the easier it becomes to do.

No Ceiling on Metaphors

WHENEVER stakes are high and passions deep, you will see metaphors from widely different sources being used to capture the essence of what's happening.

Here are some examples of commentary about the U.S. debt ceiling debate in August 2011 from the worlds of:

Factories & Fireplaces

Belinda Luscombe interview with ex-GOP Senator Alan Simpson, *Time*, 8/8/11)

Time: "How bad is it? Could the U.S. become the next Greece?"

Simpson: "As my pal Erskine Bowles [co-chairman of the deficit-reduction commission] says, 'We're the healthiest horse in the glue factory.'"

Time: "What's the biggest obstacle to cutting the deficit?"

Simpson: "The absolute rigidity of the parties ... Somebody said they're as rigid as a fireplace poker but without the occasional warmth."

Mythology

(James Surowieki, *The New Yorker*, 8/1/11)

"...One argument you hear for having a debt ceiling is that it's useful as ....a 'pre-commitment device'—a way of keeping ourselves from acting recklessly in the future, like Ulysses protecting himself from the Sirens by having himself bound to the mast."

Gambling

(John Waggoner, Kathy Chu, *USA Today,* 7/25/11)

"James Giulano of Vibrant Investment Group thinks ... the dollar could fall dramatically ... gold could soar to $1,900 to $2,000 an ounce soon .... 'Hopefully, the Democrats and Republicans can figure something out,' he says. 'It's like they're playing Russian roulette.'"

Children's Games

(Natalie Bendavid, Carol E. Lee, *The Wall Street Journal,* 7/29/11)

"The debt crisis has arisen because most Republicans and some Democrats are refusing to support a debt-limit increase unless it is linked to sweeping deficit cuts. But they can't agree on the nature or scope of those cuts—and that leaves them in a staring contest, each insisting the other blink first."

The Take-Away

Metaphors to make your points can come from any source. Think beyond the more commonly used worlds of sports and war to surprise your audience and make your points more memorable.

Tigger or Eeyore?

WHAT is one of the costliest mistakes a company can make? Hiring the wrong person for a job.

When I was General Manager of a leading communications firm in NYC, I interviewed a candidate for a sales position. I initially felt good about this person, but as the conversation continued I realized he would be disastrous in the job. At one point, he mentioned that he loved theater. Since I share that passion, I asked an unusual question: "If you were to describe yourself as a dramatic genre, which would you be?" Without missing a beat he answered, "Tragedy." When asked why, he explained, "Tragedy captures the essential existential nature of man. Like King Lear, for example, tragedy reminds us that we cannot control our destiny, that we are no better than footballs being kicked around carelessly in life by the fates."

And I was looking for a gung-ho, upbeat sales person to crack new accounts. Needless to say, whatever the merits of his view on theater, this otherwise attractive candidate did not get the job.

A metaphor saved me from a hiring error and, inadvertently, saved this candidate from what would most likely have been failure on the job.

Get the Fit Right

John Osborn, CEO of the global advertising agency BBDO, was interviewed in *Selling Power* magazine. When asked about the type of people the agency hires, he turned to images. He said he looks for individuals who are "radiators," not "drains," "hand-raisers, not finger-pointers." Team players, collaborators, sharers, forces for positivism and support—all that distilled into succinct visual language.

Mindy Grossman, CEO of HSN, Inc., which includes the Home Shopping Network, when interviewed in a *New York Times* 'Corner Office' column, said she only hires "Tiggers." She needs energy-givers. "You don't hire Eeyores." Cheerful, outgoing, confident people versus sad and gloomy downers—all captured by a metaphorical reference to Winnie the Pooh.

If You Are a Candidate

Everybody puts their best foot forward in an interview. Everybody's resume shouts experience and accomplishment. Everybody's reference letters glow with praise and appreciation. So how does a candidate separate him or herself from the competition?

One candidate, when asked by an interviewer why he should be hired to sell that firm's professional services, got the job by replying, "I'm just like Rocky. You knock me over and I come right back for more." Determination, persistence and energy—everything a sales manager could want in a new hire, wrapped up in a metaphor. No wonder he got the job.

The Take-Away

Hiring the right person is perhaps the single most important step a company can take as it scales itself for growth. One creative aid in that process is the use of metaphor. Getting agreement from management on the right metaphor, or description of a job, will save employers a tremendous amount of recruitment time and effort. And if you are applying for a job, a strong metaphor to describe your value will get you remembered in an interviewer's mind. A match in metaphors reflects congruency between employer and employee in values, focus, spirit, and business approach. All other things being equal in terms of experience, a match in metaphors is a win for everyone.

Ride That Cyclone!

MARY Anne Doggett, Managing Director at Interactive Communications is a diehard Metaphorian. In her sales classes for mutual fund wholesalers, she asks participants to describe their funds, and she shows no mercy when they produce uninspired answers. As each one expounds on the virtues of their particular funds, she challenges them with, "And what makes you different is...???!" At which point, in defense, they repeat what they just said—but louder—as if reciting the same litany of facts with even more vigor will make them sound more distinctive than the first time around.

Mary Anne tells them, "You have to be kidding if you think anyone is going to remember all the facts you just stated. Let's try something different."

She then puts the group into teams and instructs them to "paint a picture" to convey what their firms do. The ground rules are: they may not use any facts or numbers. This turns out to be difficult for people who think they look smart rattling off pages of process and performance data. According to Mary Anne, for the first few minutes they freeze like deer caught in the headlights.

Then they begin. Initially they recite clichés like, "We help smooth out your ride." But with a little prodding from Mary Anne, they start to create more original and more memorable images. One wholesaler came up with, "Have you ever ridden or seen the Cyclone roller coaster? You know the excitement of approaching the top of the ride and then the awful sinking as you plunge down on the other side? Well, we make sure you never have those extremes in your portfolio."

Other wholesalers come up with fresh analogies that fit their selected prospects. That concept of smoothness and consistency can be expressed in many worlds, depending on what the advisor knows about his prospect. For example, for prospects interested in:

- Cooking: "Have you ever cooked a dish that had too much spice in it, and it ruined the whole meal? We make sure all the ingredients in your portfolio are blended together to produce just the right investment results for you."
- Fishing: "It's one of those activities where some days you can hit it big and others come home empty handed. We make sure you get a steady catch over the long term."
- Raising kids: "There are days when your kids are wonderful and can do no wrong, and days when the opposite is true. What's important is that they turn out okay in the end. We take care of your investments with the same goal in mind, making sure they turn out okay to meet your retirement needs."

The advisors leave Mary Anne's seminar with the insight and tools they need to tailor their stories to the interests and personalities of their prospects.

The Take-Away

Mary Anne's thesis is that what stops most people from using imagery to simplify and clarify their messages is the misguided notion that lots of facts and data makes them look smart. But too much information has the opposite effect—it confuses the audience and drives them away. When people are overwhelmed with information, they rarely make a decision—or admit they don't understand. Only when people feel emotionally connected to you do they experience a level of trust that helps them make the decision to buy.

3. Once Upon a Time

It's a Small, Small, World

WHEN he was Vice President of North American Field Sales at Yahoo!, Mitch Spolan would regularly take up the mighty pen in his internal sales newsletter to make important points for his team. Here is one story he wrote:

On a recent trip to Sunnyvale, I found myself craving a half decaf, half regular, iced coffee with a squirt of vanilla, a couple sugars, and some half-and-half. Yum. It was the end of the day, so I grabbed my bag and headed downstairs to URLs [our local café].

The place was empty … except for one table. There was my friend Dave Z. who called me over to say hello to three people I didn't know. It turns out the three other people were from Akamai [an internet company], and I was scheduled to have a meeting with one of them the following week. We hadn't met in person yet. Dave had to leave, and I stayed to chat for a bit. The woman, Kristen, explained that she actually lived in San Francisco. She asked me where I lived. The rest of the conversation went something like this …

Mitch: *Atlanta*
Kristen: *Really!? My family lives in Decatur.*
Mitch: *No kidding! I actually live in Decatur too. It's just easier to say Atlanta because no one knows Decatur. It's so small.*
Kristen: *Wow! Yeah, my family lives in Oakhurst [neighborhood in Decatur].*
Mitch: *No way! I actually used to live in Oakhurst! My son goes to Oakhurst Elementary. It's across the street from us.*
Kristen: *YOU'RE KIDDING! My niece goes to Oakhurst Elementary!*

At this point, our voices are getting louder with each response. And my voice? Well, it's getting squeakier.

Mitch: *NO WAY!*
Kristen: *YES! My family lives on …. Avenue!*
Mitch: *NO!! I USED TO LIVE ON …. AVENUE!*

Kristen:	*YOU'RE KIDDING! They live at 232 .... Avenue!*
Mitch:	*I can't believe it! I lived just a couple doors down. At 303 ....Avenue!!*

At this point, her eyes BUG out of her head. She grabs her purse, fumbles through it, finds her Blackberry, frantically punches a few keys and WHIPS it around pushing it two inches from my face. It reads...

Jennifer...
303 .... Avenue
Decatur, GA 30030

Uh huh. Wait. There's more.

Kristen:	*My PARENTS live at 232 ... Avenue... My SISTER lives at 303 .... Avenue!!!?*
Mitch:	*YOUR SISTER IS JENNIFER M....????????? I bellowed!*
Kristen:	*"YES!" she screams*
Mitch:	*YOUR SISTER OWNS A SPEECH THERAPY PRACTICE!!!?!?!*
Kristen:	*"YES!" even louder this time!*
Mitch:	*NOT ONLY DOES YOUR SISTER LIVE IN MY FIRST HOUSE, THE HOUSE WHERE I LAID THAT BLACK AND WHITE CHECKERBOARD FLOOR IN THE KITCHEN, THE HOUSE WHERE I BUILT THAT PICKET FENCE, THE HOUSE WHERE I HUNG ALL OF THOSE MAPLE CABINETS AND INSTALLED THAT PEDESTAL SINK...YOUR SISTER IS MY SON'S SPEECH THERAPIST!!!!!!!*

We hugged.

What are the odds of meeting someone randomly in URLs, who lives 2,500 miles away from me, whose sister lives in my first house and is my son's speech therapist? Well, according to the 2000 US Census, there were 105,500,000 households in the USA in 2000. Let's just say 1 in 105,500,000 is being generous.

Two things here ...

- *First, it's a small world. Small, SMALL world. You will bump into friends, and friends of friends your entire life and will continually be amazed at how everyone is interconnected.*
- *Second, "brands" are transferable. I love Jennifer M.... She is gentle and kind, smart and honest. She is fun to be around and a great member of our community, not to mention a great speech therapist. Because I love Jennifer, I now default to liking Kristen because Jennifer's "brand" is so solid with me. If I didn't like Jennifer, I likely would not give Kristen the benefit of the doubt.*

Business works the same way. When our CEO [Carol Bartz] does what she did this week, kicking ass during interviews with Kara Swisher and CNBC's Jim Goldman, your "brand" got a bit stronger because of what she did. The next time your client sees you, they may feel a little differently towards Yahoo! because of Carol. When you go above and beyond for a client, you are helping everyone else at Yahoo!'s "brand" get stronger because that client thinks more highly of the work we do. Remember, it's a small world. You never know where that client will end up.*

Brands are transferable. Be a good person. Build your brand, and our brand too. You never know who you might meet in URLs.

The Take-Away

Since this was written, Carol Bartz was forced out of Yahoo! two years later, but that doesn't detract from Mitch Spolan's profound understanding that stories used as metaphors are timeless springboards from which to make your point. Stories capture our attention and keep us engaged. They give us pleasure and relax us into listening, which means we're less likely to see the pitch or advice coming and feel defensive.

Stories can come from anywhere. Possibilities include things your children do and say; experiences you have while traveling; conversations you have with people at conferences or elsewhere; something you read in the paper or on the Internet; interactions with people you meet in the street, on the train, in a restaurant, or anywhere.

Be alert and alive to the many threads that make up the fabric of your day and reweave them into metaphorical stories to make your points fresh and colorful.

Bait Your Blog

MARY Anne Doggett, the source for the earlier "Ride That Cyclone!" story, offers another excellent example of the use of

*Carol Bartz became CEO of Yahoo! in spring 2009, shortly before this was written.

metaphor to achieve a goal, but this time, the metaphor is a short memory with story-like qualities to draw readers into her blog.

> *I remember being a kid after a big snowfall, up to my knees in white fluff, dragging my flexible flyer sled up the hill. On the first run, I always needed a shove from behind to conquer my fear. After that I was happily making a running start myself and flying with the wind.*
>
> *It might just be me, but I see lots of senior executives still at the top of the mountain. The snow has fallen. They have made the difficult trudge up the mountain. And yet they are still waiting to make any decisions to move forward. Afraid perhaps of an Olympic crash? It is hard to tell. A small handful have gone ahead. For the rest, the snow is beginning to melt and they might never get to ride like the wind.*
>
> *Moving forward takes a leap of faith and sometimes a shove from behind. It may mean spending money, making investments, and taking risks. Some people are still standing in place, waiting for some sign of safety before they make the leap. They'll likely be standing there a long time.*
>
> *What will it take to see that making the investment now is the only way to see how far you can go?*

The Take-Away

Engagement online is king. In the busy blogosphere, a short opening story guarantees both instant engagement and a frame for the key point of your post. Notice also Mary Anne's powerful use of descriptive detail which makes both the childhood scene and the executive dilemma even more vivid.

The Tall Poppy Syndrome

ONE of the occupational challenges of being a professional speaker (in addition to having to consume a lot of bad airplane food) is the need to come up on the spot with good answers to unexpected questions from an audience. Susan RoAne, known as "The Mingling Maven,"® and the author of *How to Work a Room* shares this experience.

My area of expertise is networking. On one occasion, I was speaking to a mixed generation group on how to work rooms, events or gatherings when 'Joe,' a young man starting out in his career, raised his hand.

"What if you do all those things you've just mentioned and your friends poke fun at you?" he asked.

His question took me by surprise, since no one had ever asked that before. Joe knew how to socialize and comport himself, and yet he was getting grief from his peers. I could hear the genuine confusion in his voice and knew my answer had to be carefully worded and definitely not glib.

The audience was looking at me, waiting to hear a response that met their approval. I went blank ... thinking how best to answer. Then, I remembered an experience I had in New Zealand and used that to solve the problem.

I said, "Joe, your question reminds me of the time I was coaching an emerging author and speaker and she said that in New Zealand those who stood out (or above the crowd) were often cut down, both verbally and by actions of jealous people. Apparently in that country, no one likes the Tall Poppies that rise above the field."

I continued, "Her comment made me remember a time during my teaching career when my supervisor used his version of the Tall Poppy image. After I had done a particularly good job teaching a class, he advised me to be more 'low-key,' basically telling me to be less outgoing than I am. Even then, I knew that such toe-the-line thinking only leads to mediocrity in results—and I was having none of it!"

I concluded, "You are so fortunate to be comfortable around people in any room and to be able to socialize easily. But you must never be less than who you are in order to make those who aren't as good at what you do feel better. Hiding your mingling and socializing talents won't make them any better at these skills, and it will only work against your own interests."

"We are not in New Zealand. Be proud to be that Tall Poppy, to be who you are, and to stand tall in any situation."

My response to Joe satisfied both him and the audience and I continue to use the Tall Poppy metaphor whenever I'm coaching reluctant or fearful aspiring authors and those who want to improve their socializing and networking effectiveness.

And Joe, wherever you are, I thank you for asking me that question.

The Take-Away

Personal emotionally filled experiences that are universal work effectively in handling potentially sticky communication situations as long as they resonate with your audience.

Susan's use of the Tall Poppy metaphor succeeded on three levels. First, even though Joe caught her off guard, she was able to come up with a strong answer to his question. Second, by sharing a personal recollection of feeling vulnerable, she strengthened the connection to her listeners. Third, her response re-focused the group on her networking lesson. She accomplished all that with the simple, but powerful story, of the Tall Poppy.

The PIN Code

(From Doug Weaver, Founder & CEO of Upstream Group and author of "The Drift," a digital marketing industry blog. Below is a recent post.)

> *If you're like me, when you're in need of cash in the middle of a busy day, you're not all that picky about where you get it. My eyes scan the horizon for three simple letters: A-T-M. I don't much care about the brand and color scheme of the cash machine, or whether it's Chase or Bank of America or People's Bank or HSBC. All I know is, when I punch in the right set of numbers, money comes out and I'm on my way. And while this cavalier approach to personal bank interaction works out pretty well, it also provides an unflattering metaphor about the relationship most of us have with ad agencies.*
>
> *Often during my workshops, I'll quiz a group of digital sellers about the agencies they regularly call on. I inquire about the agency's mission and the key selling points it uses to pitch new business. I ask about its operating principles and values. And I'm also curious about the quality and duration of its relationships with key accounts: Are they fresh? Healthy? Aging? Troubled?*
>
> *Most of the time these questions are met with embarrassed silence and averted eyes, because all too often the agency is nothing more than an anonymous ATM machine. Pay no attention to the brand or the color palette: just punch in your numbers and wait for the cash.*

The truth is, when you call on an ad agency, you're actually selling to two businesses. Yes, it's ultimately the client's money that's being spent, but it's foolish to overlook the business objectives of the customer's agent—the agency. The shops you call on are businesses in and of themselves; they strive to build brand cultures, grapple with self-identity, struggle to motivate their people, and seek competitive advantage over their other agencies. But do we take any of that into account when we're considering our approach? Or are we just punching buttons?

Here's a simple quiz to underscore my point. Consider five top agencies: Starcom, Digitas, Universal McCann, PhD and OMD. In its mission statement, one talks about 'smart analytics combined with world class technology.' Another points to 'a culture of thought leadership, creativity and innovation.' This one is all about 'curiosity.' That one says 'experience design is the future.' Yet another calls itself 'an integrated agency with a brand core.' Could the members of your sales team collectively match each agency to its statement of values? I have to think that with just a little digging—with just a little curiosity—sellers could know far more about the shops they calls on, increasing their own value and personal brand at the same time.

The most common complaint I hear from sellers about agencies is their tendency to commoditize the sales offerings, to take a simplistic, one-dimensional view of what sellers have to offer. The shoe may not feel especially comfortable on the other foot, but there's little doubt it fits.

The Take-Away

Doug is an acknowledged thought leader in the digital world. As an industry gadfly, he constantly challenges his followers to re-fresh their business practices. It is no surprise that he uses metaphor to help change how his readers "see" their opportunities.

4. Beginner's Success

Engage Me or Die

BILL Burns works at Broadcom Tech Publications and is a self-described "mild-mannered technical writer" by day, and a "communications nut" by night. Convinced that technical presentations did not have to be as boring as the ones he was constantly seeing, he recently decided to take to the soapbox himself and deliver what he believed to be a model presentation at his firm's huge All Hands event.

"I thought my first presentation was all ready to go several weeks prior to the event," writes Bill, "And then I listened to one of your recorded webcasts on the power of metaphor and realized my presentation was just yak, yak, yak, with no real engagement, and NO metaphor. So I completely reworked it, focusing on the brain as the key target of a good presentation. ('Your brain remembers what engages it, and doesn't remember what doesn't engage it'). Then I seasoned the whole thing with a healthy sprinkling of engaging metaphors."

"Not only did it succeed as a presentation in itself, but it turned everybody into critics: throughout the rest of the week, my colleagues were commenting to me about the other presentations we saw and how they measured up according to the structure I had taught them! As I'm sure you know, nothing's better than watching your input go viral!"

Here are three examples from Bill's presentation ...

- *When I first started applying to companies fresh out of college, my dad said, 'Don't contact the HR department, because one of their jobs is to keep you out so that the people who are in can do their work without you getting in the way.' Your brain is your HR department. One of its jobs is to keep stuff out that's not important so you can work with the stuff that is important....*

- *Densely packed slides are visual overloads. When a presenter stands in front of an audience and talks over densely packed slides, it creates auditory overload. Brains hate overloads. When brains get overloaded, something disastrous kicks in: the School of Fish Syndrome.*

  Small fish travel in big schools to avoid being eaten by sharks. The sheer number of fish makes it almost impossible for the shark to focus on any one of them. So instead of a feast, the shark goes away famished. Like the shark, when our listeners are confronted with a sea of ideas from our slides and our voices, they cannot focus and they go away from our presentations remembering almost nothing.

- *...Present one idea and one simple graphic per slide. This allows your slides and spoken words to work together—engaging your brain more effectively than either one could do alone. This is the perfect presentation blend. And just like us, brains love a perfect blend.*

The Take-Away

It needn't take a long time to get up the metaphor making curve. With a little thought, you, too, like Bill, can change "Yak, yak, yak" into "Yes!, Yes! Yes!"

JFK, Zorro, or Wonder Woman?

OCCASIONALLY we are called upon to speak before audiences that are out of our norm. That can mean toasting the bride and groom at a wedding, or delivering a eulogy at a funeral. In Jim Sayers' case, it meant delivering a sermon from the pulpit of his church when his pastor was called out of town.

Jim lives in Humbolt, Iowa, and he decided to base his sermon on Hero Worship in reference to Mark 1:14-20—when Christ recruited disciples Simon, Andrew, James, and John, asking them to follow him, and then have others follow them.

Jim knew the topic well, but he thought, "How am I going to engage this congregation?"

He began talking about the heroes we worship today, those individuals that we respect and look up to, who make us want to be like them and follow them.

He continued talking about how we have heroes throughout our lives—beginning when we're kids and our heroes are the ones on our pajamas and lunchboxes, and who we dressed up as for Halloween. Later in life he said that our heroes are "real" people such as musicians, movie and TV stars, scientists, athletes and political leaders. As adults, we come to realize that our heroes do not necessarily have to be superstars, but can be normal, ordinary people whom we respect to inspire us.

"As I spoke," reports Jim, "I could see people nodding with the understanding that comes from recalling personal experiences. Eighteen or eighty, they were each thinking about the arc of personal heroes they had admired from childhood on. Not only did I have their attention, but I knew my analogy had succeeded in helping them imagine how the disciples felt about Christ when they chose to follow him."

It was a short leap from that opening analogy to his ultimate message—that we all have the opportunity to become heroes to others.

The Take-Away

Even something as innocent as a story about childhood heroes can become the gateway to a serious message. Listeners immediately recall their associations and emotions attached to those heroes, and when they do, their engagement meter goes straight up.

Did you begin to think back to your own childhood heroes as you read Jim's story? Me, too.

5. *News You Can Use*

Arab Spring

PRIOR to meeting with a prospective client, Lynn Hutzel-Visel, VP Institutional Trust at Comerica Bank, happened to read an article in *World* magazine that compared the West's historical treatment of Egypt to that of parents who continuously look the other way when their fractious teenager repeatedly acts out, only to wake up one day to find themselves with a seriously destructive child on their hands.

"My client was stuck in a state of inertia about whether to buy our services," Lynn recalls. He thought he could just continue going along with the small setbacks he had been experiencing in the market. He did not want to face the consequences of not moving ahead. Remembering the article, I said to him, "There comes a time, as it does with any parent who ignores the ultimate effect of permissiveness, when, if you don't become pro-active, it all tends to blow up in your face."

Perhaps he had children and could identify with the analogy, or perhaps he simply saw the truth of it. Whatever it was, Lynn reports that the comparison changed his perception of the issue and kicked him into action.

The Take-Away

Current events from wars, the environment, and the Olympics, to drug smuggling, famous weddings (divorces), scientific discoveries, and even terrorism, offer a daily bazaar of metaphors, any one of which can be adapted to make your point in meetings.

Your next metaphor is only a newspaper read away.

Blood Is Quicker Than Water

I HEARD this story around Halloween, so talking about blood seemed appropriate. Lots and lots of blood. Being harvested from one human being after another, dripping into rows and rows of plastic bags…

Bad opening to a horror movie? No. The happy ending to a story from the South Texas Blood Bank drive.

Gayle Prettyman works as Publications Specialist at the San Antonio Blood & Tissue Center. Their job is to recruit blood donors. "Donations are usually down during the summer months," she says, "so we really needed to encourage people to donate." In addition, "Texas was in a severe drought and everyone was talking about the absence of rain."

That combination of her need and the weather conditions on everyone's mind led her to come up with a winning metaphor, one that ultimately solved the blood bank's problem:

"Water isn't the only lifesaving resource we need this summer.

Donate blood."

"We tweeted that phrase," Gayle reports, "and the ripple effects were terrific. Our area water system re-tweeted it, so an entirely different group of people heard the message. In addition, newspapers used it as the opening line in our press releases that talked about blood needs and upcoming drives. As a result, the blood bank got its donors."

Bloody good ending, that was.

The Take-Away

Gayle's metaphoric line brilliantly yoked together water and blood as lifesaving resources, while leveraging the topicality of the drought. The seeds of successful metaphors can be found not only in the big news of the world, but also in what's happening in your community.

President Obama's State of the Union

HOW do you sell your idea of unity to an audience that is diverse, divided, and, in many cases, downright hostile to you and your views?

That was President Obama's challenge in his 2012 State of the Union address. As you read the following, notice how he:

- Sets up his theme with a story.
- Reviews the accomplishments of the troops working together.
- Describes the values they demonstrated.
- Contrasts their single-minded success with the splintering in current politics.
- Then uses the success of military unity as his guiding metaphor for the unity that could rescue America's future.

The result is an emotionally engaged audience. With the theme set, his audience is ready to hear the details.

Last month, I went to Andrews Air Force Base and welcomed home some of our last troops to serve in Iraq. Together, we offered a final, proud salute to the colors under which more than a million of our fellow citizens fought—and several thousand gave their lives. We gather tonight knowing that this generation of heroes has made the United States safer and more respected around the world. For the first time in nine years, there are no Americans fighting in Iraq. For the first time in two decades, Osama bin Laden is not a threat to this country. Most of al Qaeda's top lieutenants have been defeated. The Taliban's momentum has been broken, and some troops in Afghanistan have begun to come home.

These achievements are a testament to the courage, selflessness, and teamwork of America's Armed Forces. At a time when too many of our institutions have let us down, they exceed all expectations. They're not consumed with personal ambition. They don't obsess over their differences. They focus on the mission at hand. They work together.

(Link to his theme) *Imagine what we could accomplish if we followed their example.*

Think about the America within our reach: A country that leads the world in educating its people. An America that attracts a new generation of high-tech manufacturing and high-paying jobs. A future where we're in control of our own energy, and our security and prosperity aren't so tied to unstable parts of the world. An economy built to last, where hard work pays off, and responsibility is rewarded.....
(Theme Repeated in Summary)
...which brings me back to where I began. Those of us who've been sent here to serve can learn from the service of our troops. When you put on that uniform, it doesn't matter if you're black or white; Asian or Latino; conservative or liberal; rich or poor; gay or straight. When you're marching into battle, you look out for the person next to you, or the mission fails. When you're in the thick of the fight, you rise or fall as one unit, serving one Nation, leaving no one behind.....

So it is with America. Each time I look at that flag, I'm reminded that our destiny is stitched together like those fifty stars and those thirteen stripes. No one built this country on their own. This Nation is great because we built it together. This Nation is great because we worked as a team. This Nation is great because we get each other's backs. And if we hold fast to that truth, in this moment of trial, there is no challenge too great; no mission too hard. As long as we're joined in common purpose, as long as we maintain our common resolve, our journey moves forward, our future is hopeful, and the state of our Union will always be strong.

The Take-Away

Was the speech too long? Maybe. Did the audience agree with everything the President said? Certainly not. But did he creatively and emotionally set up his argument, and get people to listen? Definitely. And he did it through storytelling, a powerful theme, and the extensive use of imagery. When the stakes for an audience's hearts and minds are high, vivid visual language is a winning strategy.

6. It Doesn't Have to Be Dull, Trite, & Boring

A Cliché a Day Keeps a Buyer Away

IF ever there was a more overused and empty claim in sales than, "We partner with our clients," I would like to hear it. First of all, what would you be doing if you weren't "partnering" with clients to solve their problems? Second, "partner," "partnering," and "partnership" have so much mileage on them that they have about as much persuasive traction as a set of bald tires on a muddy country road.

So how do you make the idea of partnership come alive?

Patrick Thornton, Sales Representative for Centro.net, does it with a simple metaphor.

Centro.net offers media logistics services that make it easy to manage the many aspects of buying digital media. The company operates in a complex space in which buyers often have a tough time not only distinguishing the value of one service from another, but also understanding what it is these companies offer in the first place.

Says Patrick, "When it comes to explaining how we partner with clients, I like to say that Centro.net and its clients are like rowers on a boat. When all the rowers are aligned in motion and are moving fast, it leads to great velocity. Centro works to constantly align with our clients' goals. Our cutting edge technology and expertise in the digital space also generates communication speed with clients, so Centro helps you work faster and do more with your day. This fresh image for what partnership means gives buyers a vivid impression of how working with us truly helps them achieve their goals."

The Take-Away

Look at your proposals. Look at your presentations. Replay what you typically say on sales calls. What phrases do you repeatedly use that could be replaced by a visual metaphor that has greater impact? Look for tired phrases like *Turn-key, Full-service, #1, Best in class, Bible of the industry.* These points need to be made, but make them pop for clients with original images.

Down by the Seashore

HOW do you take a topic that is pretty dry and humdrum and make it feel new and compelling? Lynda Decker, President of Decker Design in New York City, faced that dilemma when she was asked to design the annual report for natural gas provider New Jersey Resources. The company prides itself on being environmentally friendly, but words like "green" and "greening" have been so overused they sound like clichés. Also, natural gas isn't a topic people are eager to read about.

"We decided to play off New Jersey's well known shoreline and create a beautiful teal blue brochure that metaphorically illustrated the message New Jersey Resources wanted to convey. The combination of message with visual imagery really delighted our client."

Starting with the cover, the report captures the reader's attention immediately with a picture of a little girl with a pail and shovel walking along the beach. The title of the annual report: *Conserve to Preserve: The Wave of the Future.* (Theme set)

The opening line expands on the theme: "*Like the perpetual motion of the ocean tides that stretch along the coastal communities of our service territory, change is constant. It happens every moment of every day. Sometimes it happens in waves. Other times change happens in ripples, so slowly and incrementally that it is hardly noticed at all. How we rise to the challenges created by change separates the great from the good and the truly accomplished from the merely acceptable. It's what makes an effective company an enduring one that will stand the test of time.*"

The theme links to their business. *"Fiscal 2008 was a year of immense change and daunting challenges for our country..."*

The photo spreads throughout the report metaphorically reinforce the details in each section:

- Title: *Preserving Our Future.* Image: A boy building a big sandcastle.
- Title: *Leading the Way.* Image: Footprints in the sand along the water's edge.
- Title: *Delivering Reliability.* Image: A dad tossing and catching his son in the air on the beach.
- Title: *Meeting New Challenges.* Image: A person in a small bright yellow boat riding a beautiful blue wave.
- Title: *Achieving Results.* Image: A fisherman with a huge catch.
- Image only: The closing page concludes with a picture of a lighthouse with a bright beacon showing the way.

The Take-Away

When presentation topics are dry, a visual theme will immediately move that information from the mundane to the memorable. By using powerful imagery throughout the report, Lynda transformed a seemingly dull company into a strong and friendly ally of the environment.

What Color Is Your Hat?

ONE of the challenges to problem solving is that we are creatures of habit and tend to "see" things the same way each time we look at them. That patterned thinking is very useful for routine living, when, for example, we automatically know to stop our cars for red lights and to go ahead on green, or, when we recognize the right child to pick up from school. Imagine if you had to stop every time you came to a traffic light to figure out what the color meant, or wander through a schoolyard asking every kid which one was yours.

However when it comes to problem solving, looking at a problem the same old way is likely to yield only the same old answers, which are unlikely to cast a fresh light on the situation. And when you work as a team, you probably know that much time can be lost as people argue from their unique perspectives: *"I think we should do..." "But I feel we should..." "Hey, wait a minute. We don't even know..." "You're forgetting..."*

Edward De Bono, world renowned creative thinking guru, helps people solve this problem in an orderly way by inviting them, metaphorically, to try on different thinking "hats." You can use his efficient approach alone or with a group:

By yourself, you run through the hats in your own mind in order to reach a solution. In a group, everyone is asked to wear the same hat at the same time, and the discussion progresses through the different colors, OR, participants can be assigned different color hats and then contribute to the discussion according to their color.

The different colored hats are:

- White: What are the facts? What information do we have about the situation?
- Red: How do we feel about this situation?
- Black: What isn't working? Why?
- Yellow: What is working? Why?
- Green: What are the possibilities? What can be done differently?
- Blue: What are our next steps?

The colored hat metaphor not only gives clarity and structure to a problem-solving meeting, it also adds fun. Try it yourself or with your team the next time you're faced with a problem.

The Take-Away

Edward De Bono's six hat metaphor made a complex process with many moving parts easy to understand and to do. You can employ a similar strategy for your explanations. Use a physical object for the different factors, drivers, processes, or elements of your subject. For example, you can use a stool to represent the three legs of a successful sales organization; a glove with each finger representing an element of a new business plan; a train with each car representing one step in a process; a car with each wheel representing a technical factor in a system; a meal with each course representing the beginning, middle, and end of a service. The possibilities are limited only by your imagination. Simply identify the number of components you want to present. Then select the best physical object to represent that number to make those components both meaningful and memorable for your listeners.

7. *Take Them Out to the Ball Game*

What Inning Are We In?

HOW many times have you walked out of a sales call and weren't quite sure of your chances for winning the business?

Chris Hogan, a recent presentation seminar participant, has a highly effective way of solving this problem. Chris calls on media buyers at advertising agencies in New York, and his Internet firm has a longer than usual sales cycle. He recalls: "I was out meeting with clients from a leading pharmaceutical company, and our client was a big Yankees fan. We had been negotiating for the past couple of months and I wanted to know where we stood in the decision buying process vis-a-vis the competition. So, I asked, 'If we're on 1st base, is anyone on 2nd and 3rd base?'"

He responded, "No."

(If he had said yes, I would not have liked it, but at least the game would have gotten interesting. Knowing others were "on 2nd or 3rd base" would open the opportunity to refresh the client on why we were better.)

"Great," I said, "So we are currently leading the game. It sounds like we are in the top of the 7th. Is that an accurate statement?" (I always use 7, as most sales forces use a CRM tool on the % likely to close business, so 7th inning could mean a 70% chance of being selected.)

"More like the bottom of the 7th," he said, "But you are definitely in the lead."

"When I hear that," continues Chris, "I can continue the metaphor in different ways. For example, depending on the situation, I might say, 'So how much longer to this game until it ends?' or, 'Glad we are in the 7th inning. My team and I are focused on getting to the end of the game and would like to do the following, etc....'"

"Putting the developing business relationship in the context of 'innings'" says Chris, "makes it easier to gauge where I am in the sales cycle and how to move the prospect forward to a commitment."

The Take-Away

Metaphors can finesse asking difficult questions. In this example, the baseball metaphor was non-threatening, because Chris's client was a baseball fan. The metaphor also provided a framework for creating momentum towards action. This works for Chris at each point in his relationship with the client.

Caveat

Do not use baseball metaphors if:

A. The top and bottom of anything only makes you think of fashion, and ...

B. Your listener is not a baseball fan.

Metaphors and analogies work only when the language and imagery are familiar to both speaker and listener.

Batter Up!

IN this age of email and texting, the handwritten note is a much-appreciated rarity

Suppose you are a venture capitalist in the process of taking over a company. Not surprisingly, the employees are resistant. Discussions have been going on for quite a while. At the final critical meeting, the President does an outstanding job of supporting you in front of the employees. You sit down to write him a personal thank you note. You know he is an ardent baseball fan and decide to tap into his love for the sport.

Bob,

I wanted to thank you personally for this exciting opportunity. The company is a diamond in the rough, and I hope to help it become a brilliant gemstone for you. Lots of work to do, great help and support from the whole team. Barb, Michael and Sal are the best batting line up any pitcher could hope to have on his team. I will undoubtedly have a few walks, but hopefully more strikeouts than balls, and I know we can win this game with you as the coach.

My sincere thanks for this great opportunity. I know I will see you lots of times before the ninth inning, but feel free to come out to the mound anytime you want to talk.

Warmest regards,

Joel

The Take-Away

A little over the top for you? Maybe, but not for Bob. He loved the genuine thoughtfulness, humor, appreciation, and optimism dressed up in the language of his favorite sport.

Find out your clients' passions. Use that imagery to hit home runs when you're writing congratulatory or thank you notes.

8. *Spontaneous Eruption*

Where Is the Next Party?

(CNBC Closing Bell. May 13, 2011)

CHRISTOPHER J. Cordaro, CFA®, CFP® and Chief Executive Officer and Chief Investment Officer of RegentAtlantic Capital surprised CNBC Closing Bell hosts Bill Griffeth and Mandy Drury on their show with the way he explained that RegentAtlantic Capital had been out of commodities all year long, well before the recent significant downturn in commodity prices. Cordaro quipped, "I'd rather leave the party early and have less of a hangover on the way down."

His response prompted Drury to ask, "Chris, if you like to leave the party while things are pumping, Lady Gaga's playing, everyone is lying on the floor...what would you be getting out of now?"

Cordaro responded, "We're out of commodities and REITs, but what I think is really interesting is to ask, 'Where is the next party? Oddly enough, we think the next party is in Europe. If we look at European stocks, they're selling incredibly cheap relative to the rest of the world because of the sovereign debt crisis hanging over it. You want to buy them when they're cheap, and before the party's over, you want to sell them to somebody else."

(The interview continued with a further discussion of the various asset allocation changes RegentAtlantic had made since September 2010.)

When I congratulated Chris afterwards on that metaphor, he told me it came to him "spur of the moment." It was no surprise to me that the party metaphor just popped into his head, because metaphors are so much a part of our daily thought process. Drury's pick-up on the party theme injected new energy and color into the conversation and turned a fairly routine exchange into a lively and memorable discussion, engaging the listeners and scoring extra points for RegentAtlantic Capital.

The Take-Away

Don't be surprised when strong metaphors and analogies pop up spontaneously in your conversations. You use these communication tools unconsciously all the time: "It's raining cats and dogs." "They fell in love." "It takes two to tango." "Don't bite off more than you can choose." "Send it by snail mail." "X is the white elephant in the room."

Try this experiment: Keep track of how many times you hear and use metaphors during the day. The number will surprise you.

What's a Ferrari For?

HOW many of your clients buy the full range of your services or products? Probably fewer than you would like. It is frustrating to be aware of what clients could be getting in value if only they would invest more with you, not to mention how much better it would be for your bottom line.

That was Kelsey's situation. Kelsey worked for a high profile financial services firm. He dealt at very senior levels in *Fortune* 500 companies. He was a seasoned expert who enjoyed his work and had excellent relationships with his clients. But it bugged him that many of them paid premium prices, yet didn't do more business with the firm.

One day he became so frustrated with the client that he blurted out, "Look, Joe, you're paying for a Ferrari in our service and all you do is use it to drive to the grocery store. That's not what a Ferrari is for!"

To his surprise, the client stopped to consider what that really meant and then began a conversation to explore broader ways to use the Ferrari services Kelsey's firm offered.

The Take-Away

When we are frustrated or angry, we sometimes swear. But when swearing is not appropriate, we often find ourselves reaching for a metaphor to express our feelings. For example:

1. Angry mom to teen: "What do you think I am—your maid!?"
2. Frustrated driver stuck in traffic to friend on cell: "I'm sitting in a damn parking lot!"

Get angry enough and the perfect metaphor will generally pop out.

9. When Idols Fall

Humpty Dumpty Woods

Tiger Woods sat on a wall.
Tiger Woods had a great fall.
All of his billions and all of the spin
Couldn't put Tiger together ag'in.

I'm no competition for Mother Goose. But if you have ever doubted the power of metaphor, just look at Tiger Woods. In a few short days, he went from being admired as an elite performer and worldwide role model to being the poster child for scandal, shame, and personal failure.

A marketer's dream, Tiger Woods with his handsome looks and whistle clean image made millions for companies like Accenture ("Go on, be a Tiger"), Gillette, and Nike. They all basked in the metaphoric glow of his reputation. And he, of course, made millions for himself as well.

Now "Go on, be a Tiger" will forever be the punch line to some lame joke—which explains why his former sponsors all dropped him.

The Take-Away

What's in a metaphor? Everything.

10. When It's Personal

Twist the Kaleidoscope

EVER notice that every once in a while a client can be a bit, shall we say, unreasonable?

One participant in a "Got Metaphor?" seminar I was leading shared two effective ways of dealing with demands from these people—both making use of powerful metaphors. Linda works for a tech company and had a client, Richard, who wanted to get a quality product from her firm in an impossibly short amount of time. He suggested her firm add more staff to get the product out the door faster.

Linda explained that wouldn't change anything. Richard ignored her comment and insisted that adding more staff was the answer. Exasperated, Linda finally said, "Listen, Richard, you can't give three different women three months each and get a baby. Some things require more time and process stages to develop effectively. This is one of those things." Richard had nothing to say after that.

On another occasion, this same client also wanted a test right away, but did not want to discuss the specifications and requirements. Realizing by now that logical arguments didn't do the trick with Richard, Linda once more tapped into the world of metaphor. She got Richard to cooperate by pointing out, "If you tell a builder to build you a house and provide no further details, you will not end up with a house that you are pleased with or that meets your needs. You may get a house, but you will likely have spent a great deal of money and not be happy with the final product. That is why we need to discuss the details on this project before doing your test." Richard thought for a moment and then agreed to provide the necessary information.

The Take-Away

For whatever reasons, clients, colleagues, even friends can make ridiculous demands on us. When logic fails, give their mental kaleidoscopes a metaphorical twist. As the little glass pieces of your metaphor fall into a fresh pattern in their minds, the new way of looking at the situation will work to everyone's benefit.

Picking a Few Bones

ALEXIS was retiring from a job she'd held for many years, and she wanted to say goodbye to colleagues of longstanding. She wrote:

To my fellow colleagues,

It is with mixed emotions that I leave you to retire to a life that is all about family and friends. I am hoping you will remain part of this circle. It's been a wonderful experience working with you and I wish you every success this world has to offer. Keep up the enthusiasm and the good work!!

But before I go, I need to pick a few bones with you. I want to pick ...

A Wishbone—I wish you everything that is good. May you live life to the fullest, have loved ones and dear friends to support you, and may you achieve all that you hope for while avoiding doing harm to anyone.

A Funny Bone—I hope you laugh when life gives you lemons, realizing that work is only a small part of true happiness. I hope you learn to laugh at yourself and at the silly things/people that annoy or frustrate you. Find humor even in the most difficult of times. Try and stay positive, remember the good times.

A Back Bone—I hope you have the courage to stand up for what you believe is right and speak your mind. To deliver what the clients need rather than what they want. To work with integrity and forthrightness. To have the courage to create an atmosphere of honest feedback.

My time at this company has been filled with incredible experiences, wonderful memories, and the opportunity to work with the best and brightest colleagues I could imagine. Everyone on the Executive Coaching Program has been invaluable to my growth, and for that I am grateful.

All the best, with warmest regards,
Alexis

The Take-Away

Alexis' metaphor sets up a clever and charming way to both categorize and expand on her thoughts. Creating a triad of "bones" adds a pleasing rhythm to her message as well. A triad works well in any situation where there are multiple buckets of ideas, services, or options from three pieces of advice to a college graduating class, to three types of services you offer to clients, to three kinds of growth strategies for an organization. Our brains like the music inherent in groups of three (A,B,C; One, Two, Three; Tom, Dick & Harry, beginning, middle, end). Package your metaphors in threes and your message is guaranteed to resonate and be remembered.

I hope these stories and tips have convinced you of the power metaphors can play in getting what you want, what you need, and what will meet your goals. I encourage you to release your inner Metaphorian and, then, watch what happens.

Chapter Notes

Chapter 1: The Challenge: Getting Heard

1 Hayakawa, S.I. *Language in Thought and Action.* New York City: Harcourt, 1991.
2 Lederer, Richard. *The Play of Words: Fun and Games for Language Lovers.* New York City: Pocket Books, 1990.

Chapter 2: What Are Metaphors?

1 Source unknown.
2 "McCain's Mutiny." *Fortune.* 3/7/03.
3 "Past Private, Future Public." *Forbes ASAP.* 10/5/98.
4 Conference call with reporters. 3/19/93.
5 "Shares of Distressed Firms Still Sell." *The Wall Street Journal.* 1/22/03.
6 "Music to Our Ears." *Playbill.* 3/28/03.
7 Stoppard, Tom. *Rosencrantz and Guildenstern Are Dead.* New York City: Random House, 1967.

Chapter 3: When Do You Need Metaphors?

1 "Prostitutes Preach Condoms." *The New York Times.* 1/4/98.

Chapter 4: Your Audience's Brain Craves Metaphors

1 As reported in Nelson, Noelle. *Winning! Using Lawyer's Courtroom Techniques to Get Your Way in Everyday Situations.* Paramus, NJ: Prentice Hall, 1997.
2 Advertisement. *Business Week.* 6/18/01.
3 Heimel, Cynthia. *If You Can't Live Without Me, Why Aren't You Dead Yet?* New York: Perennial, 1992. A very funny book.

Chapter 10: Beware Bad Metaphors!

1 "Where the Smart Money is Flowing." *Fortune.* 5/25/03.
2 Levitt, Arthur. Heard on *Bloomberg Radio.* 4/30/03.
3 Cited in Ivers, Mitchell. *Guide to Good Writing.* New York City: Random House. 1991.
4 "Grinding Axis." *The New Yorker.* 2/11/02. Very interesting, longer exposition of this topic.
5 "Future Perfect." *The New Yorker.* 10/20-27/97.
6 "Getting Beyond Downsizing." *Fortune.* 1/10/04.
7 Letter to Editor. *Business Week.* 11/3/97.
8 "It's Not Just Social Security." *Business Week.* 10/26/98.

Chapter 12: Grabbers: Get Attention

1 "Dreaming Out Loud: One Tiny Little Tax." *The New York Times.* 2/2/03.
2 "Blurbage." *Business 2.0.* 6/26/01.
3 Daly, James. Editor's Page. *Business 2.0.* 5/15/01.
4 Told to me by consultant David Wethey, Agency Assessments. London, England.

Chapter 13: Anchors: Position Yourself

1 "No Preservatives, No Unions, No Dough." *Fortune.* 9/15/03.
2 "Brand Yourself an Expert." *Inc. Magazine.* 6/04.
3 "Powerfest: When Tech Stars and Moneymen Meet." *Fortune.* 1/11/99.
4 Di Monteemolo Cordero, Luca, CEO Ferrari. *BusinessWeek.* 3/8/99.
5 "Go Dog Go!" *Fortune.* 5/12/03.

Chapter 14: Nutshells: Make Memorable Recommendations

1 "America's Secret Weapon." *Business 2.0.* 12/01.
2 Speech given by Sam Hill. 92nd Street Y Marketing Forum. New York. 2003.
3 Becker, Gary. "Economic Viewpoint." *Business Week.* 5/26/03.

Chapter 15: Burners: Explain, Simplify, Reinforce Points

1 "Can Sallie Save City, Restore Sandy's Reputation and Earn Her $30 Million Paycheck?" *Fortune.* 6/9/03.
2 Advertisement. *Fortune.* 6/9/03.
3 Reuters. The Latest News. 11/17/01.
4 Weaver, Doug, President, Upstream Group. *The Drift,* his online newsletter. 3/17/03.
5 "The 'But' Economy." *The Wall Street Journal.* 10/30/03.
6 "Is It Time to Let Learning Styles In?" *Training.* 5/02.
7 "This is Brain Surgery." *Fast Company.* Feb/Mar. 1998.
8 Heard at a Victory Capital Investment Management meeting. Cleveland, Ohio.
9 "The Hottest Thing in the Sky." *Fortune.* 3/8/04.
10 "When Dinosaurs Mate." *The Wall Street Journal.* 1/22/04.
11 "Farenheit 9/11 Is Raising Conservatives' Temperature." *The Wall Street Journal.* 6/30/04.

Chapter 16: Shockers: Make Numbers Stick

1 *The New Yorker.* 4/26/03.
2 *Strategy & Business, First Quarter.* 1999.
3 Letter to Editor. *Selling Power.* 7-8/97.

4 "Comment." *The New Yorker.* 6/10/02.
5 "What's Wrong With Us?" *Time.* 1/2/89.
6 Can be viewed online as a short, powerful and beautiful movie, "The Miniature Earth," produced by Lucca Co.: http://www.perspectivesaustin.com/earth.htm

Chapter 17: Seducers: Titles That Tease

1 "Recipe for a Best Seller: Analogies About Cheese or Anthills or Parenting." *The New York Times.* 9/01.
2 *Business Week.* 1/12/04.
3 *The New York Times.* 4/26/98.
4 *Fortune.* 3/8/04.

Chapter 18: Sledgehammers: Headlines That Hit Home

1 Advertisement. *Fortune.* 3/17/03.

Chapter 20: Props: Add Impact

1 "Yahoo Outlines Plans for Adding Premium Services." *The New York Times.* 2/13/03.
2 Reported in a book review of John Kotter's "The Heart of Change." *Strategy + Business,* 4th Qtr. '02.

Chapter 22: Observe and Connect

1 www.thinkingcoach.com/lincoln/lincolnquotes.htm
2 "The Expanding Entertainment Universe." *Business Week.* 8/14/95.
3 Carlin, George. *brain droppings.* Hyperion. New York. 1997.

Chapter 23: Travel to Other Worlds

1 Lederer, Richard. *Op.cit.*

Chapter 24: Become a Clipper

1 Safire, William. "To Fight Freedom's Fight." *The New York Times.* 1/31/02.
2 "The Economy Under Siege." *Fortune.* 10/15/01.
3 Op Ed. *The New York Times.* 9/5/01.
4 "The Telecom Depression/When Will It End?" *Business Week.* 10/7/02.
5 "Hurling Derision and Goat Spoor on a War Movie Bomb," *The New York Times.* 3/2/03.

Bibliography

American Press Institute. *Effective Writing and Editing.* Reston, VA: API, 1985.

Buzan, Tony and Richard Israel. *Brain $ell.* New York City: McGraw-Hill, 1997.

Carter, Rita. *Mapping the Mind.* Berkeley: University of California Press, 1999. The most beautifully illustrated and best written book on the brain. Highly recommended.

Christ, Henry I. *Winning Words,* 2nd ed. Boston: D.C. Heath and Co., 1966.

Cialdini, Robert. *Influence.* New York City. Wm. Morrow & Co., 1984.

Clurman, Ann. Smith and J. Walker. *Rock of Ages.* New York City: Harper Business, 1997. Excellent for understanding the markers and values of today's different generations.

Crystal, David and Crystal, Hillary. *Words on Words: Quotations About Language and Languages.* Chicago: University of Chicago Press, 2000. A wonderful addition to the library of anyone who takes joy in the art of wit and language.

Davenport, Thomas and John Beck. *The Attention Economy.* Boston: Harvard Business School Press, 2001. Excellent analysis of how difficult it is to get and keep attention in today's world.

Dowis, Richard. *The Lost Art of the Great Speech.* New York City: Amacom, 2000.

The American Biology Teacher 49, 417-420 Digiovanna "Make it Meaningful and Memorable."

Gibbs, Raymond W. Jr. *The Poetics of Mind.* Cambridge: Cambridge University Press, 1995.

Hayakawa, S.I. *Language in Thought and Action.* New York City: Harcourt, 1991.

Khatena, Joe. *Imagery & Creative Imagination.* Buffalo, NY: Bearly LTD, 1984.

Lakoff, George Mark Johnson. *Metaphors We Live By.* Chicago: University of Chicago Press, 1981.

Lederer, Richard. *The Play of Words: Fun and Games for language Lovers.* New York City: Pocket Books, 1990. Lederer's books are highly entertaining to read for language lovers.

Mills, Harry. *Artful Persuasion.* New York City: Amacom, 2000.

Noelle C. Nelson, Ph.D. *Winning! Using Lawyers' Techniques to Get Your Way in Everyday Situations.* Paramus, NJ: Prentice Hall, 1997. One of the best books ever for salespeople.

Ortony, Andrew. *Metaphor and Thought.* Sec. Edition. Cambridge: Cambridge University Press, 1993.

Pinker, Steven. *How the Mind Works.* New York City: WW Norton & Co., 1997.

___________ *The Language Instinct.* New York City: William Morrow, 1994.

Plotnik, Arthur. *The Elements of Expression.* Lincoln, NE: Excel Press, 1996.

Poor, Edith. *The Executive Writer.* New York City: Grove Weidenfeld, 1992.

Restak, Richard. *Mozart's Brain and the Fighter Pilot.* New York City: Harmony Books, 2001.

Richards, I.A. *The Philosophy of Rhetoric.* New York: Oxford University Press, 1936.

Rose, Colin and Malcolm J. Nicholl. *Accelerated Learning for the 21st Century.* New York City: Dell Publishing, 1997.

Rostand, Edmond. *Cyrano de Bergerac.* New York City: Bantam Books, 1954.

Rupp, Rebecca. *Committed to Memory: How We Remember and Why We Forget.* New York City: Crown publishers, 1998.

Russell, Peter. *The Brain Book.* New York City: Penguin Books, 1979. Extremely informative, entertaining, book on the subject.

Seyba, Mary. *Imaging: A Different Way of Thinking.* Hawthorne, NJ: Educational Impressions, 1984.

Sommer, Elyse and Weiss, Dorrie, editors. *Metaphors Dictionary.* New York City: Gale Research, Inc.,1995. This is a large book arranged like a dictionary by topic from Abandonment to Zenith. Most entries are historical and literary and only occasionally useful for business and speeches. Worth a look at the library before buying.

Spence, Gerry. *How to Argue & Win Every Time.* New York City: St. Martin's Press, 1995. Excellent not just for its relevance to this topic, but for overall psychology of persuasion.

Stumpf, Stephen, Joel DeLuca. *Learning to Use What You Aleady Know.* San Francisco, CA: Berrett-Koehler. 1994.

Williams, Roy H. *Accidental Magic.* Atlanta, GA: Bard Press, 2001.

____________. *Magical Worlds of the Wizard of Ads.* Atlanta, GA: 2001.

Wolf, Michael J. "The Battle for Your Attention." *Strategy & Business.* Q1. New York City: Booz-Allen & Hamilton. 1999.

Wurman, Richard Saul. *Information Anxiety 2.* QUÉ. Indianapolis: 2001.

Other Sources of Interest

For quotations on any topic, there are numerous book collections readily available at your local bookstore. Online, there are numerous sites that will provide quotations from many fields, individuals, and sources. Use popular search engines like Yahoo! and Google and type key word "quotations"

www.famousquotations.com

www.anecdotage.com—A search engine for anecdotes, the range of topics is breathtaking.

www.americanrhetoric.com—A search engine for great speeches. Spend some very fascinating time learning how the great historical communicators used language to persuade their audiences.

www.cartoonbank.com—Sells cartoons from *The New Yorker* on a wide range of topics.

www.dc.com—Bullfighter: Stripping the Bull Out of Business. A very amusing website.

www.introknocks.com—Sells sales greeting cards many of which use metaphors for a variety of sales/client correspondence.

Schenkman, Richard. *Legends, Lies and Cherished Myths of American History.* NY: Harper and Row, 1988. An offbeat source for unusual stories that could be the basis for a metaphoric opening or closing.

Wright, Larry. *Happy as a Clam and 9999 Other Similes.* New York City: Prentice Hall General Reference, 1994.

Aesop's Fables, Edith Hamilton's Mythology, Grimm's Fairytales, The Bible—all can provide excellent short stories to make a point.

About Anne Miller

Anne is founder of Chiron Associates, Inc. For the last twenty-five years, she has specialized in sales and presentation skills seminars, speaking, and consulting for high profile associations and *Fortune* 1000 companies, both in the United States and around the world. She has appeared on Bloomberg News Radio and CNNfn and has been featured in numerous online and offline publications and as a guest lecturer at Columbia Business School. She is the author of "Make What You Say Pay!" "365 Sales Tips for Winning Business," and "Presentation Jazz!" Anne holds her MA from The University of Wisconsin and resides in New York City.

For More of Anne Miller Online and In Print

1. Subscribe FREE to:
   "Make What You Say Pay!," a weekly blog that challenges your thinking about selling and presenting in a very noisy world.
   "The Metaphor Minute," a short, monthly online newsletter featuring a metaphor cleverly used in business or from the news for you to use now or store for future use.
2. Give **"The Tall Lady..."** to friends, staff and colleagues *Single* copies available online at Amazon and Barnes & Noble, or order from your local bookstore.
   Quantity orders & discount information. Please see next page.
3. WIN a free book or special report
   Send a brief story of how you used a metaphor to (A) sell your product, service, or idea; (B) overcome confusion or resistance; or (C) dramatize a point.
   Submit entries as often as you like: *amiller@annemiller.com*
   Winners chosen monthly!

Order Form

For quantity orders (10+) and publisher discounts,
call BookMasters at 800-247-6553

Single copies may be ordered from popular online bookstores
and from http://atlasbooks.com

or you may use the order form below:

Name ______________________________

Company ______________________________

Mailing Address ______________________________

City & State ______________________________

Telephone ______________________________

Fax ______________________________

E-mail ______________________________

Please send__________copy (copies) of ***The Tall Lady with the Iceberg*** @ $15.95 per copy.

Please bill my credit card.

Credit Card: ☐ Visa ☐ MC ☐ Amex

Card # ______________________________

Expiration Date ______________________________

Signature of Cardholder ______________________________

Code________ (last three digits on back of credit card)

Please mail your order form to:

BookMasters, Inc.
30 Amberwood Parkway
Ashland, OH 44805
800-247-6553

You may fax your order to: 419-281-6883
E-mail your order to: order@bookmasters.com

Please add $4 shipping and handling.
Ohio and New York sales taxes are applicable.